True Life in God

Vassula

Volume Six

(Notebooks 59-64, part of 65)

Published by

Trinitas™

Declaration

The decree of the Congregation for the Propagation of the Faith, A.A.S. 58, 1186 (approved by Pope Paul VI on October 14, 1966) states that the Nihil Obstat and Imprimatur are no longer required on publications that deal with private revelations, provided they contain nothing contrary to faith and morals.

The publisher wishes to manifest unconditional submission to the final and official judgment of the Magisterium of the Church.

True Life in God

Vassula

Volume Six

(Notebooks 59-64, part of 65)

Published by

Trinitas™

P.O. Box 475
Independence, Missouri, USA 64051
Phone (816) 254-4489

Copyright © 1993, Vassula Ryden

ISBN: 0-9631193-9-7

For further information direct all inquiries to Trinitas.

Cover photo: from Agamian Portrait, courtesy of Holy Shroud Guild.

Printed in United States of America.

Also available in Spanish, French, Italian, German. Translations in progress include Greek, Danish, Russian, Portuguese, and Japanese. For information contact Trinitas.

Welcome

To the praise of Jesus and Mary

In reading the messages, always read Volume One first and follow the order of the books so that you become immersed in God's Love for you.

Jesus asked me to tell you to always take my name, Vassula, out of the messages and replace it with your own name.

I really must express here my gratitude to my family, my spiritual director, and all my faithful friends who have made the preparation of this book possible.

I want to mention Father René Laurentin, Sr. Lucy Rooney, Father Bob Faricy, Father Michael O'Carroll, Tony Hickey, Pat Callahan, Tom Austin, and everyone who promotes and helps distribute these messages. I bless the Lord and thank Him for the ears that heard His Cry of Love from His Cross and now, touched, become His mouthpieces broadcasting this Cry of Love.

The text presented in this volume is the original English. At my request, there have been some abbreviations and additions which were necessary either due to the personal nature of a message or to clarify the sense of certain passages.

Vassula

Table of Contents

Prayers Given to Vassula

Jesus to Vassula
January 29, 1990

Lord my God,
lift my soul from this darkness
into Your Light,
envelop my soul into Your
Sacred Heart,
feed my soul with Your Word,
anoint my soul
with Your Holy Name,
make my soul ready to
hear Your discourse,
breathe Your sweet fragrance on my
soul, reviving it,
ravish my soul
to delight Your Soul,
Father, embellish me, Your child,
by distilling Your pure myrrh
upon me,

You have taken me to Your
Celestial Hall,
where all the Elect are seated,

You have shown me around
to Your angels,
ah, what more does my soul ask?

Your Spirit has given me life
and You, who are the living Bread
have restored my life,
You have offered me to drink
Your Blood,
to be able to share for eternity
with You, Your Kingdom
and live forever and ever,

Glory be to the Highest!
Glory be to the Holy of Holies.
Praised be Our Lord.
Blessed be Our Lord, for His
Mercy and His Love
reaches from age to age and
forever will; Amen.

Mary to Vassula
May 15, 1990

Father all Merciful,
let those who hear and hear again
yet never understand,
hear Your Voice this time and
understand that it is You
the Holy of Holies;
open the eyes of those who see and
see, yet never perceive, to
see with their eyes this time
Your Holy Face and Your Glory,
place Your Finger on their heart
so that their heart may open
and understand Your Faithfulness,

I pray and ask you all these
things Righteous Father,
so that all the nation be
converted and be healed through
the Wounds of Your Beloved Son,
Jesus Christ; Amen.

Prayers Jesus Recommended to Vassula
(to be said daily)

Novena of Confidence to the Sacred Heart

O Lord, Jesus Christ,
to Your Most Sacred Heart I confide
this intention (state your request).

Only look upon me,
then do what Your Heart inspires,
Let Your Sacred Heart decide,
I count on It, I trust in It,
I throw myself on Its Mercy.

Lord Jesus, You will not fail me.
Sacred Heart of Jesus, I trust in Thee.
Sacred Heart of Jesus, I believe in
Thy love for me.
Sacred Heart of Jesus,
Thy Kingdom come.

O Sacred Heart of Jesus,
I have asked for many favors,
but I earnestly implore this one.
Take it. Place it in Thy Sacred Heart.
When the Eternal Father sees it
covered with Thy Precious Blood,
He will not refuse it.
It will be no longer my prayer,
but Thine, O Jesus.

O Sacred Heart of Jesus,
I place my trust in Thee.
Let me never be confounded.
Amen.

Prayer to St. Michael

St. Michael, the archangel, defend
us in the day of battle; be our
safeguard against the wickedness
and snares of the devil.

May God rebuke him, we humbly
pray, and do thou, O prince of the
heavenly host, by the power of God,
cast into hell, Satan,
and all the other evil spirits,
who prowl through the world
seeking the ruin of souls. Amen.

The Memorare of St. Bernard

Remember, O most gracious
Virgin Mary, that never was it
known that anyone who fled to
your protection, implored your
help, or sought your intercession,
was left unaided.

Inspired with this confidence, I fly
unto you. O Virgin of Virgins, my
Mother! To you I come, before you
I stand sinful and sorrowful.
O Mother of the Word Incarnate,
despise not my petitions, but in
your mercy, hear and answer me.
Amen.

Introduction

+Most Reverend Donald Montrose

Bishop of Stockton
Stockton, California

At a celebration of Christian Unity Vassula Ryden, accompanied by Father Michael O'Carroll, gave a presentation on the Messages of Jesus in the Blessed Sacrament Cathedral, Sacramento, California on January 18, 1993, the Feast of Christian Unity.

Bishop Francis A. Quinn, Bishop of Sacramento, on behalf of Mary's Peace Mass Committee, had invited Vassula to speak in his diocese. Bishop Quinn and Bishop Donald Montrose, of Stockton, California concelebrated the Monthly Peace Mass at which Bishop Montrose gave the following homily.

In the second reading today we heard the words, "In this way the love of God was revealed in us." God sent His only Son into the world that we might have life through Him.

As we begin this week of Christian Unity it is a beautiful time for Vassula to come to speak to us. And so, in a very special way, I am going to offer the Mass that I am saying tonight for Christian Unity that all of us, with all of our hearts, would ask the Lord for this great gift.

When we think of the truths of the Gospel, we see the great, great love that Almighty God has for us. We hear the words of St. John's Gospel: "God so loved the world that He gave His only Son." We are called upon to really believe in this great love that God has for us. We know that the love of God and the justice in God are equal; they are both Infinite. I once saw a picture of an angel that had two faces; one looking one way, and one looking the other way. This angel represented both the mercy of God and the justice of God. They are equal. We can't fully understand God, but we know that now is the time of God's mercy. Both the mercy and the love of God are such incredible gifts to us.

After the sin of our first parents, there was created between us and God, a chasm greater than the chasm from here to the moon. There was just this infinite distance, this huge chasm, that had been created by our first parents' rejection of God. We had inherited this infinite distance from God as a result of our original sin. For us to try to bridge this chasm was impossible. It would be like trying to build a bridge from here to the moon. Absolutely impossible! Yet God so loved the world that He gave His Son. In the Incarnation of the Son of God this infinite distance is bridged, so that God and man became one in the Divine Person of Jesus Christ when He became man.

This was such an unbelievably great gift for us because everything changed once Jesus became man. God became our Father. He was not a Father to us before. In the Old Testament we never hear God spoken of as a Father, but this is how Jesus taught us to pray. He taught us to pray to God as our own Father. He is our Father who loves us and He is really a Father to us.

In these messages from Vassula we really see how much God wants to be our Father, how much He wants us to love Him, and to be His children. It is such a great gift that the Lord has given us through the Incarnation. In many ways He gives Himself to us especially in Holy Communion, in the Eucharist. He wants to be our Brother, and He is, in a real sense, a Brother to us.

This, I think, is the message that I would hope that all of us would carry home tonight, the message of the great love of God, because if we really believe in this love, it makes a great difference in our lives. Sometimes, after we have sinned, we want to keep God at a distance because we believe that we are not worthy. It's true, we are not worthy, but that doesn't really matter. He is ready to forgive us, and we need to really throw ourselves on His mercy and love and accept that love into our hearts.

We come to know the love of God more and more. The more we pray to Him the more we are able to feel His love. We also see the great love of God and the love of Jesus in giving to us His Mother. She is really our own Mother. She is truly our Mother. You know, over there on that wall there is a picture of Our Lady of Guadalupe. The message of Our Lady of Guadalupe is simply that she is Our Mother. She told Juan Diego the message that she wanted to give to all of us. She said, "I am your Mother. Come to me. Come to me, because I am your Mother. I will help you. I am your Mother. Come to me, trust in me." This, too, I think, is very much the message of Our Lady in our time. The beauty of the rosary that we say is seen in the "Hail Mary." In that prayer, in a very real sense, when we say "Hail Mary" we are asking Mary to pray with us. She prays with us to the Father, and she really wants to show herself as a Mother.

So, let us keep with us the great realization of the love of God for us and the knowledge that we have a real Mother, the Mother of Jesus. May we always remember that Jesus with practically His dying breath gave her to us so that she would be our Mother, and so that we might truly love her as a Mother. Again I say, if we take those messages to heart we will continue to be greatly blessed.

A Letter from Bishop Montrose

When Bishop Montrose of the Diocese of Stockton, California placed an order for books and videos, in August, 1992, we asked that he share his response and insights with us. We were very pleased when we received the following which he has graciously allowed us to reprint:

Truly, it would not be appropriate for me to make a judgment on the writings of Vassula Ryden, and I submit anything that I say to the judgment of the Church.

From a personal standpoint, I can only state that what I have read in the first volume of *True Life in God* has been of real benefit to me. The writings have given me new insights into the incredible love that Jesus has for me personally, and for each one of us. They have led me to a greater faith and trust in that Divine Love.

I hope and pray that many others will also be blessed by reading *True Life in God*.

+Donald W. Montrose
Bishop of Stockton

Preface
+Frane Franic, Retired Archbishop of Split
President, Episcopal Theological Commission, Yugoslavia
Split, Yugoslavia

When I received two books written by the visionary, Vassula Ryden, and translated into Croatian by Mrs. Marija-Dragida Vukic, I was pleasantly surprised, all the more because the translation was made from English in Belgrade, where Mrs. Vukic lives. She asked me to write a preface for the third book which will appear in Croatian. There are already five volumes in English entitled *True Life in God* written by Vassula Ryden. It is a great pleasure for me to write this preface.

The first news I heard about Vassula was two years ago, in 1991, in a Canadian Catholic review, *L'Informateur Catholique*. A great deal of that particular issue was devoted to Vassula. Thereafter, the review published information about her regularly. A good Catholic lady living in Canada, who is very interested in Medjugorje, a leader of frequent pilgrimages, directed strong criticism against Vassula, alleging that there were false theories in the messages which she is transmitting: for example, that Jesus calls Himself "Eternal Father" of men, as if He identifies Himself in every respect with the Father, thus denying the distinction between the Father and the Son. This devoted admirer of Our Lady is not happy either with the manner in which Jesus transmits His messages through Vassula's hand; she thinks of this in terms of spiritualistic transmission of messages.

This critic of Vassula, about whom I read in the review I have mentioned, was Mrs. Darija Klanac, nee Skunca. I had the honor to meet her on her way as a pilgrimage leader from Canada to Medjugorje. She visited me in Split, in St. Peter's Co-Cathedral, where I have lived since 1983. I spoke in French to the pilgrims about the Medjugorje messages of peace. Mrs. Klanac also talked with great zeal about Our Lady.

I was very happy that Mrs. Klanac, one of our Croatians married in Canada, had such a high reputation among the Catholics of that country. Later on, when she had difficulties with the review I have mentioned because they supported Vassula, I noticed with what respect they wrote of her personality, that is, the experts working for them. This pleased me.

But I am on Vassula's side, especially since I was given three books of her messages in Italian, entitled *Peace and Love*. A group of Italian pilgrims on their way to Medjugorje stopped in Split and visited St. Peter's. They invited me to Italy. So, on September 23, 1992, I celebrated Holy Mass in a large church in Como. The church was full and there I met Vassula. Before Mass she gave a testimony about her mystical experiences and messages, which, with the greatest conviction, she attributed to Jesus. I gave the homily on the Gospel of the day. I spoke about private revelations, and the importance they have for the Church and today's world. I added some words of support for Vassula, leaving the final judgment to the Church. I always use this precaution when I talk publicly about the Medjugorje messages.

On the other hand, when I talk privately I express my constant conviction of the authenticity of the Medjugorje apparitions and messages; I rely on the Gospel test which says that a good tree may be recognized by good fruits. This is especially true of religious conversions, miracles in the moral order, and, most frequently, experiences in Medjugorje. This happens also through Vassula, who herself is a miracle, an object of wonder. True, she does not cause wonders in the physical sense, for she makes no claim to a charism of healing.*

I was given a copy of the fourth book of Vassula's messages by the translator personally. I was delighted to note that the preface was by Fr. René Laurentin, whom I value highly; I have met him many times in Split on his way to and from Medjugorje.

As I read Vassula's books, my first impressions of her were very much confirmed. Her messages, actually for me Jesus' messages, are alive and authentic. These messages can help us toward a better understanding of Jesus' messages in the Gospel, and also help us experience them in a personal way. These must always remain the authentic criteria in judging private messages, in recognizing healthy mystical experience. There always have been, always will be, mystical experiences in the Church. These we must not minimize, but we must leave the final judgment to the church.

When I met Vassula in Como, on 23rd September, 1992, I had the feeling that she was under attack by many critics; they wrote disparagingly about her. This is understandable as through Vassula, Jesus is passing judgment on extremist theologians of our time, who distance themselves from divine revelations by too great proximity to the world. This Pope Paul VI found out, a short time before he died; he began to speak of the "devil's smoke" which had entered the Church and clouded fundamental truths of God's revelation.

It seems to me the more I understand these things, that Vassula's main charism is to show the PURITY OF THE INTEGRAL REVELATION OF GOD. Nothing must be taken from, nothing added to, the Revelation; there must be no yielding to the world and to the permissive civilization of our time, which penetrates even into the Church, causing disorder in her saving mission.

Inculturation is necessary as the basis of a new evangelization. So Pope John Paul II says,

following the Council. We must respect all cultures that we may plant in people of all nations God's revealed truths, strengthening them with love, always with due regard for human, national and social rights, and attention to social situations. This is the truth; the Second Vatican Council says it; so do the Popes of the Council and after it. But there is the truth which tells us that Christ and His Word judge all cultures, all human, national and social rights. It is not, on the contrary, the cultures which judge Christ, but Christ who judges them. Christ protects, promotes, dignifies, raises to a higher level, to God's level, all cultures.

Because of that do not be afraid to "open the door to Christ." He is our Creator, our Friend. He is our "Eternal Father" together with the Father and the Holy Spirit; He knows what we need to achieve our small earthly and great heavenly happiness.

The Church, together with the Pope, and under the Pope, as the visible head of the Church and the Vicar of Jesus Christ, transmits the saving teachings of Christ. That is what Jesus is telling us through Vassula, though she makes it clear that she is of the Greek Orthodox Church. In this way she shows the way to healthy ecumenism, ecumenism which, today, is passing through its Calvary. But ecumenism is God's work, so it must pass through its Calvary like Christ Himself. May God protect us so that the Calvary does not spread over the whole world.

Ecumenism will, through its Calvary, have its resurrection. It seems that this is the core of all the messages that Jesus is giving us through Vassula Ryden, Greek Orthodox, living now in Switzerland.

*To respect the record, it must be stated that healing has taken place more than once during prayers at her meetings.

Foreword
Echo of the Gospel
Rev. Ljudevit Rupcic, OFM
Theologian, Professor of Exegesis, Author
Zurich, Switzerland

Every day Vassula Ryden has a new experience of the divine; she continues to spread her prophetic message in today's world which is increasingly more remote from God, remote from the foundation on which it is established, risking its very existence. Vassula is a true prophet of our times. On the one hand, she deals with the problems and the needs of our times; on the other hand, she seeks new prospects from God, to come finally enriched from her difficulties and find in Him harmony, peace, and fullness. Her message is imbued with the Gospel. Its special feature consists only in the way of transmitting it to us; besides, Vassula offers to the old and new problems of our world nothing but the everlasting Gospel.

Vassula is, like all other prophets, convinced of the truthfulness of her message and the authenticity of her mission. She knows her own weakness but she resolutely keeps to her commitment to diffuse the message to others. She finds God's help in continuous prayer and in the Eucharist. Persevering in her will and desires, she strives to be entirely united with God. She is conscious of the urgency to diffuse the message because time is running out and an inescapable great chastisement is looming; it can be avoided only if we come back to God, and accept Him again.

Vassula's experience with God is a lasting and inexhaustible spring of wisdom, love, enthusiasm for God and the salvation of the world. For that reason the testimony is convincing, joyful, and stimulating. Besides conversion and a call that humankind should answer love with love, there is also concern for church unity. "Love loves you" (3/7/92) means that, in Vassula's talks and union with God, each one of us can and is allowed to, put himself or herself in Vassula's place. God loves everyone in that way. Everywhere in her writings we feel the Breath of Love. Grace flows everywhere; the Holy Spirit is everywhere at work, giving profusely. Everywhere one hears the Lord's steps.

Vassula's writings are an echo of the Gospel. The One who speaks is, indeed, the very Word of God. Most readers and listeners recognize in His words the voice of God (14/7/1992). Vassula does not tell anything basically new that God would not have already told, but God's Word is brought up to date through her mouth, giving prominence to priorities and needed emphasis. In this way the Word is actualized, serious, convincing, a testimony.

The question, "Why repeat what has already been said?" means that one does not know the needs of humankind, who have the right to hear God's Word in an understandable, updated way. Besides this, there is the obligation to become a messenger of the Word, which gives testimony within human experience. Due to the forgetfulness of men and women, one too easily overlooks the forthcoming disaster and the immediacy of the catastrophe to which mankind is exposed; it is necessary to take it out of this indifference so as to allow grace to flow continuously and to foster conversion.

Despite the objective authenticity of Vassula's testimony, people, here and there, raise objections to its truth. Though they are not sufficient to call the testimony in question, the reasons are both of an objective and subjective nature. Reservations arise mainly from a narrow and fragmentary view of the mystery of grace, especially when grace is poured out gratuitously, grace whereby God makes the human person a partner in his life and of his works. All these objections amount to human notions and language because they come from a limited human experience, unable by its limitations to accept the mystery of God. Hence man questions the Word of God and refuses to accept God. For the skeptic the Word of God is always too difficult, even "scandalous," and consequently taken as untrue. The initial assumption of the human mind should be to accept the fact that things which cannot be perceived do exist, and to this one should remain open. It is only in openness to God's grace that human beings can attain a sure, valuable and adequate knowledge of the mystery.

Criticism arises from the fact that Vassula's experiences and testimonies are not in harmony with the ignorance and prejudice of those who are prisoners of their own imagination. Vassula's testimonies are witness against the false understanding of those who disparage her, not against the Gospel or the faith. In no way is she against the God of the Bible, or against faith in him. Those who disparage her are really seeing one opposed to their own way of imagining God whom they assume generally to be One seated on his Throne, far from humankind. For Vassula, human existence is capable of receiving God's love, his grace and his omnipotence. This "scandalous" view is, in reality, a rediscovery of God. It is a baseless charge to represent Vassula as a supporter of "New Age." It is as illogical as mixing fire and water. Such criticism merely shows that the critics do not know either Vassula or "New Age."

On the other hand, one should reflect on where Vassula's message would lead if it were put into practice. If people faced the reality of love in God and in men, they would be led to love God and one another. If people answered the request for prayer, the message would spread throughout the world the note of thankfulness to God. If one accepted that there must be unity between the Christian Churches, already there would be a hope of the fulfillment of Jesus' promise—"one fold and one Shepherd."(Jn. 10:16). If people accepted God the way Vassula recommends, He would already be "everything in everyone"(1 Cor. 15:28). If people took seriously Vassula's warning about Satan, the latter would already be banished from men's hearts and from the world. If people would heed Vassula's call to conversion, all men and women would be saints already. If everyone shared in Vassula's experiences, the personal history of each one, and consequently the history of all humankind, would be a Song of Love.

All this is completely in the radical style of the Gospel. On this assumption there are no grounds for separating Vassula's experiences with God from the Gospel, still less for opposing them. Vassula's messages presuppose an aptitude in human nature for dialogue. Individual believers, those especially who are rich in the Spirit, have the right to evaluate the case of Vassula, not setting themselves up independently of the Church. In this way they can support the Church's judgment efficaciously. The final judgment remains with the Church, which has its guarantee in God and His confirmation in the "sensus fidelium", of which the Spirit of Truth is the author and the witness to veracity.

All the evidence before us so far shows that every day Vassula's testimony is taken more seriously and is more fully accepted. This simultaneously facilitates and accelerates the final judgment of the entire Church, which judgment will, without doubt, take as a criteria, the many good fruits of Vassula's message.

Presentation
Howard Dee, Layman, Author
Philippine Ambassador to the Vatican 1986-1990
International Theological/Pastoral Conference Vice Chairman
Manila, Philippines

This is a great privilege which Vassula has accorded me by inviting me to write this presentation for the sixth volume of her writings dictated to her by Our Lord and Our Lady.

As an ardent student of the Fatima and Akita messages, I am delighted to find a strong correlation between these messages and those given to Vassula, which are imparted with a grave urgency and with so great a love and so much hurt as only God can feel. Consider this message on Christmas Eve of 1991:

"Write: citadel after citadel is being besieged by the Rebel. I come today and offer all mankind My peace but very few listen. Today I come with peace-terms and a Message of Love, but the peace I am offering is blasphemed by the earth and the Love I am giving them is mocked and jeered in this Eve of My Birth. Mankind is celebrating these days without My Holy Name; My Holy Name has been abolished and they take the day of My Birth as a great holiday of leisure, worshipping idols.

"Satan has entered into the hearts of My children, finding them weak and asleep; I have warned the world; Fatima's Message speaks: that in My Day I shall make the sun go down at noon and darken the earth in broad daylight. I will allow the Dragon to bite this sinful generation and hurl a fire the world has never seen before or will ever come to see again, to burn her innumerable crimes. ...

"Elijah and Moses have come already and you have not recognized them but treated them as you pleased; you have not listened to Our Two Hearts, the Immaculate Heart of My Mother and My Sacred Heart, you faithless generation ..." (NB 56:60-62)

The central themes of Fatima are very much alive in Vassula's messages: the excess with which

God loves man; man's denial of God which, if not reversed, would lead to his damnation; and the eventual triumph of the Hearts of Jesus and Mary. Who would believe, years ago, what is happening today, that the Christmas Nativity scene with the Holy Family would be banned from public places in so many countries including Canada and the United States. It is acceptable to display Santa Claus and Mickey Mouse but not the Saviour Lord whose birth is what Christmas is supposed to commemorate. Today, the courts have banned the Holy Scriptures from public school libraries but not pornographic literature. The same pagan courts have ruled it legal for mothers to kill the infants in their wombs. Jesus Himself prophesied these times when He asked: "When the Son of Man returns, will He still find faith in the world?"

The messages given to Vassula also confirm Akita's warning of a chastisement by fire, imparted with an even greater urgency than ever. When Our Lord told Vassula that he *"would make the sun go down at noon...and allow the Dragon to hurl a fire the world has never seen before,"* he was confirming the interpretation of Pope Paul VI who had said that the fall of the sun at Fatima was a warning of nuclear fire. He said that "the (Fatima) message was eschatological in the sense that it was like a repetition or an annunciation of a scene at the end of time for all humanity assembled together."

Like Fatima and Akita, the Vassula messages are intended not to be messages of impending doom, but to convey the great love that God and His Mother have for humanity, and to announce the imminent triumph of their Sacred Hearts over Satan and his cohorts. These messages are messages of hope to a world mired in paganism, atheism, and materialism. They are to let us know that the times are grave, the hour is late and the need for our total conversion is urgent. It is a clarion call to all disciples of Jesus and children of Mary to join in this battle of battles for the salvation of our souls and the survival of human civilization. We are invited to be part of this great triumph.

Yet we listen to these messages today and tomorrow we return to our old ways, seeking pleasure and profit in a material world devoid of moral, ethical and spiritual values. We do not take these messages to heart, and they become like seeds sown on barren ground. We read them without changing the way we live and the way we do not love each other, the way we scorn the poor, neglect the suffering, and ignore the downtrodden. So Our Lord, in His sorrow, laments to Vassula:

"Our Two Hearts are anointed and are living. They are like a sharp sword, double-edged, prophesying, but the rebellious spirits in this generation are recrucifying My Word, the double-edged sword, and are rejecting Our Two Hearts who speak to you today; just like Sodom's and Egypt's rejection of My messengers. This era's stubbornness has surpassed the Pharaoh's because their claims to their knowledge have become a battlefield to My Knowledge; indeed Our Two Hearts have become a plague to the people of the world."

Our response to these messages must be like that of the children of Fatima, Lucia, Francisco and Jacinta, who spent the rest of their lives consoling the Heart of Jesus and making everything they did an act of penance and reparation to the Heart of Mary. Nothing in this world is more important than our personal response to their Sacred Hearts. Our salvation and the salvation of the world is dependent on our response. The fate of humanity is in our hands.

The Fatima Symposium, on "The Alliance of the Hearts of Jesus and Mary," held in Fatima in September, 1986, was inspired by Pope John Paul II who speaks of the "definitive alliance of the Two Hearts," and was convened by His Emminence, Jaime Cardinal L. Sin, Archbishop of Manila.

Cardinal Sin later convened the International Theological/Pastoral Conference of "The Alliance of the Hearts of Jesus and Mary," held in Manila, Philippines in December, 1987, and served as the Chairman.

Howard Dee, a layman and author who has given himself to teaching the Devotion to the Hearts of Jesus and Mary, served as the Vice Chairman and delivered both the welcoming and closing addresses for the Conference.

The goal of the symposium was to promote the consecration of each individual as well as the whole of society to the Sacred Heart of Jesus and the Immaculate Heart of Mary. It was clearly a message of peace.

A Letter of Our Lord to His Church

Rev. Christian Curty OFM
Priest and Exorcist, Marian Movement of Priests
Marseilles, France

Automatic Writing Or Hieratic (Sacred) Writing?

It is widely known that Vassula writes messages that she transmits to us under the dictation of Our Lord. At that time her way of writing changes and becomes quite distinct from her spontaneous and everyday handwriting. The personal handwriting of Vassula is normally small and tense, though orderly and well controlled by her will that knows what she wants. Moreover, it is affected by her warm and very refined personality, which has a good sense of proportion. On the other hand, the handwriting of the messages is characterized by its order, its clearness, its regularity and a certain majesty. Here the personality of Vassula fades away and finally vanishes behind what, at first glance, seems to be merely a facade that is a bit rigid and artificial.

Consequently there arises the question that some people have, even though they judge positively the messages themselves. Quite legitimately, they ask themselves about the origin and authenticity of this "inspiration". Here, too, lies the origin of the suspicion of critical minds who find therein a significant argument for their objection to the messages as a whole. Thus they claim that it is a simple exploration of the psychic depths of Vassula herself. This interpretation reduces these writings to a phenomenon that is well known as paranormal writing. In that case, we would not be dealing with the Jesus of Christian faith and a revelation from Him. Instead, it would be something from Vassula's own subconscious that is gradually coming to light. Perhaps, they would say, there might even be another "spirit," in which case, it could only be an evil one.

What then are we to think of all this? Are we, in fact, dealing with a revelation of the Lord, a letter of Our Lord to His Church, or is this simply an example of what is commonly called automatic writing? Is it the hand of Our Lord that writes to us through the hand of Vassula, or rather, is it Vassula who describes for us, in a state of trance, whatever arises from the depths of her subconscious? Is she guided by a parasitic spirit whom we had best identify so as not to be deceived by one who is presented to us as coming from the Lord? In the first case we would be dealing with an inspired writing. In the second case we would be dealing with paranormal writing or automatic writing.

What is Automatic Writing?

It is a writing which involves either paranormal phenomena or some sort of divination. In our ministry as exorcists it is not rare to run across this phenomenon. The hand of someone who has given himself over freely to this sort of guidance writes by itself; it does not write by conscious thought or intelligence. Instead, it moves by an unknown force which is not subject to the will of the writer. Sometimes, in extreme cases, it is the instrument all by itself (a pen or pencil) which, by the mere contact of a finger, begins to write a message.

The message can be of a high literary value, even spiritual, or it can tend toward the bizarre, the ridiculous, or the vulgar. Sometimes it speaks of a world beyond, which is a marvelous kind of paradise, or else it can give some simple counsel to the writer, or give him a command regarding his daily, practical life. At times, it simply answers questions that are asked, whether it be its own identity: "who are you?" or whether it concerns things that tend to the dangerous area of divination. At times, automatic writing can predict future events which, in fact, can actually occur. Thus it can give rise to falsehood; it can also simply reveal an imaginary but plausible past which leads the writer to the false and heretical belief in reincarnation.

Let us ignore, here, the question of what we might call the problem of literary characteristics of automatic writing. It is quite unusual, in fact, that the speaker who, for example, claims to be Lamartine, actually writes lines of a quality worthy of Lamartine. For it is the subconscious of the subject who, though he may have some thoughts drawn from Lamartine, expresses only himself and not the well known author.

To remain within the framework of this introduction, let us also here put aside the sometimes grave risks that those incur who deliberately give themselves over to this paranormal phenomenon of automatic writing. There are risks at the level of the personality which becomes split, inasmuch as the subconscious rises to the surface, while the psychological awareness is kept in a state of slumber or as a passive listener. In extreme cases, this can result in a kind of artificial schizophrenia. There are also risks on the spiritual level where an evil spirit can take advantage of this lack of vigilance in a person and then intervene, thus taking control of the person. On the one hand, madness or a state of trance results; on the other a demonic parasitism! These are the two great dangers from which it is, at times, difficult to escape.

What about the Case of Vassula?

Now let us carefully see what is happening with Vassula. There are three situations to consider.

—In the first situation, Vassula receives a "locution" of the Lord, an interior word. She can be, at the time, in a church or a public place. If this locution is a message for everyone, she will write it down when she has gone home. It is then that her hand is guided by the Hand of the Lord and the graphological characteristics of her personal handwriting are transformed. From her personal handwriting, which is small, animated and quick, with a slight inclination to the right, it becomes an upright, well ordered, calm, transparent handwriting with no particular emotion. In any case, it is not automatic writing, for there is first of all an interior word which is then followed by the actual writing of the locution. We are not here dealing with the paranormal.

—In the second situation, there is a dictation which is made by the Master to Vassula, who simply writes down what she hears. She is then in the exact situation of any secretary to her employer. That means that she maintains her personal autonomy, her freedom, and her full contact with her surroundings. She can thus interrupt the dictation at any moment; for example, she can answer the telephone, and then take it up again where she left off. Here, too, the graphological pattern of her letters is not her usual one. Instead, it is a vertical, upright handwriting which is easy to read and always peaceful and measured in its respiration. Even though her handwriting is different here, Vassula maintains complete control of herself and the free exercise of her conscious faculties. She simply writes down, by hand, what she receives in an inner vision of Jesus and what she hears by this Voice that inspires her. We are thus far from automatic writing.

—Finally, in the third situation, which, at times, blends in with the preceding one, Vassula receives an interior light which is infused and has no clearly pronounced words. This is what mystics call a "motion" of the Holy Spirit (whether spiritual or intellectual) which has to be put in our language with precise words and phrases and can require various expressions which, at times, are lengthy. Vassula then hastens to write down this "insight" or "understanding" that she has just received in this infused way. It is then, when she begins to write in her own spontaneous handwriting, that the Lord intervenes and shapes the letters made by Vassula's hand into the beautiful handwriting of His own, as if to give this revelation a seal from on high. It is thus in no way automatic writing.

As if to convince us of this, the Lord, at times, proceeds in another way. Sometimes the messages to be communicated are quite long and the time available is quite short. Then the Lord permits Vassula to write the dictation in her own handwriting, which is alert and lively. That shows quite well that Vassula is in no way conditioned by this way of writing nor guided by some "spirit". Her spiritual "experience" has, then, nothing at all in common with the phenomenon of automatic writing.

It is Hieratic (Sacred) Writing

Let us look carefully at this calm, dignified writing, measured in its movements and continually animated by a vertical tendency. The median letters or the vowels are not crushed by the loops and staffs which, nevertheless, are dominant, and move with ease in the space which is their own, like that of daily life, although they are, at times, a bit confined in the interior of words. But the text breathes in the space that is provided.

Above all, there is a continual movement of coming and going which gives the whole an orientation from high to low and low to high. The text of the handwriting gives a vertical impression rather than a horizontal one, with a very evident predominance of the heights. There is, thus, nothing that is denied in the deep and instinctive life, but this depth is mastered and dominated by the higher faculties.

There is nothing, then, in this handwriting, that is directed to the Past, and amazingly, nothing directed to the Future, as if only the Present moment were important, or rather, as if everything is Present in a single TODAY.

There is no sign of any egocentric regression at this time. Nothing, indeed, indicates a falling back to the self; and the tendencies toward others are discreet, light, and always uplifting. There is an evident transparency everywhere of nobility, distinction, and marvelous clarity. The only thing that is important is this double upward and downward movement, which constitutes the continual interior rhythm. At times it descends to the earthly, human depths (which is the movement of the Incarnation), and at times, there is a perceptible elevation toward a superior being who can be none other than the Father.

Moreover, there is a bit of rigidity and artificiality in this handwriting where, at least at first glance, it is difficult to discern a human temperament, so sensitive and subject to changes (as one finds, moreover, in the spontaneous handwriting of Vassula). Here this dimension is continually directed on high, relativized, and disappears behind what might seem to be a mask. In fact, as it stands, this writing makes one think of Hebrew, that sacred language *par excellence*, in which God spoke to Moses and his people on Sinai to reveal their Vocation. That is why we describe this writing as "Hieratic".

What is Hieratic?

In the ancient theater, there was a mask worn by the actor to hide his human face and identify him with the *"passión"* of the person he played in the drama. Thus the individual, who was generally well known, disappeared behind whomever or whatever he represented. When Vassula writes under the dictation of the Lord, there is something like that in this writing that we can call "hieratic." She disappears—she is effaced behind the One who writes to us. Let us go even further. In the Liturgy, the hieratic gesture is preserved in the Great Oriental (Orthodox) Prayer and up until the time of the Council, it was also in the Roman or Latin Liturgy. It is a sacred, or more precisely, a sacralized gesture. It does not express a human temperament (that of the priest or of his assistants) which it arrests or constrains. It is performed by a man of flesh and blood, who has his own character, his emotions, his faults, even his nationality, but it is, first of all, a divine gesture. All that is relative to the individual himself and his social or geographic origins should be effaced behind an attitude that perpetuates itself in an unchanging way through space and time: for the hieratic gesture is beyond time. It is a gesture of God that is performed by a man. Such a gesture remains always the same through the vicissitudes of the centuries and changing climates and nationalities.

This is the cause of its apparent coldness and rigidity. Here there is a risk, for if the gesture remains unchanging, it can perhaps fail to convey the Spirit and can come to resemble a branch where the sap no longer flows. That is the reason why the Second Vatican Council wanted to revitalize the liturgical gestures, giving them again a more human character that is closer to our modern sensibilities, but always under the condition that we do not forget that they are, above all, sacred gestures and not those of the media. The Liturgy is, above all, a prayer and not theater. It is a work that is both human and divine, and it is thus not just an expression of our individual or collective sensibility. We cannot always be certain that this second risk is always carefully avoided in our conciliar liturgy.

Let us return now to the "Beautiful Writing" of the Lord, as Vassula likes to call it. It is thus a hieratic writing, in other words, a sacred writing that is without a human aspect. It is austere and not individualized, but at the same time it is clothed with such a majestic solemnity. Certainly one can see a sensibility here, but it is all directed on high. In other words, it is directed towards the spirit in man. Without taking into consideration the rational content of the message it conveys, the writing itself inspires a great peace in us to whom it is directed, radiating light and serenity. Truly this Writing is beautiful and can only be good!

What is the Reason for This Hieratic Writing?

There remains the question, why is it that, in these messages which he entrusts to Vassula, the Lord has chosen to use this hieratic writing, which, as far as I know, he does not use in identical situations. In fact, so many souls are also receiving revelations from the Lord without this way of writing.

First of all, is it truly the first time this has happened? In fact, one can ask oneself this question. Aren't the Holy Sriptures by definition a work of God, written, of course, by human hands, but under the inspiration of the Holy Spirit? It is good to recall this, for there are many times in Revelation where God himself makes use of the hand-written Scriptures to conserve the message and to better spread it, and above all to engrave it in our hearts of flesh.

That is what happened to the prophet Habakkuk who, like us, was troubled by the astonishing silence of God before the supplications of his people and the flood of Evil. He decided that: "I will take up my post...watching to see what the Lord will say to me, what answer he will make...Then Yahweh answered and said: 'Write the vision down, inscribe it on tablets to be easily read, since the vision is for its own time only: eager for its own fulfilment...if it comes slowly, wait, for come it will, without fail...the upright man will live by his faithfulness.' (Hab. 2:1-4) Compare also in the Apocalypse, the "letter" of the Lord to His seven Churches; Write to the angel of Ephesus...." (Ap. 2:1). Note, too, this unexpected and very meaningful interruption: "When the seven thunderclaps had spoken, I was preparing to write, when I heard a voice from heaven say to me, 'Seal the words of the seven thunderclaps and do not write them down.'"

Even if one cannot say that in these cases God himself was writing by the hand of his prophet, there are nevertheless two cases where this is explicitly said.

In fact, isn't it God Himself who, by the hand of Moses, engraved the Ten Commandments on a hard rock to engrave them on the hardened hearts of his people? These Ten Commandments were "written by the finger of God" (Ex. 31:18), but of course it was through the hand of Moses. This is proven by the words: "Cut two tablets of stone...and I will inscribe on them." But God says to Moses "Write the words yourself...and God inscribed on the tablets the words of the Covenant, the Ten Commandments" (Ex. 34:1, 27-28). Although we have not seen these two tablets engraved by the hand of God through the hand of Moses, it is clear that the typographical nature of the letters, their "Script" was in the Hebrew language, thus hieratic or sacred, depersonalized. They did not reflect the human temperament of Moses. Instead they reflected the power and the transcendence of God, who was not only the One who inspired them but also quite precisely the author; as it says, "God wrote...." Finally, we should also remember that Jesus Himself, the Man-God, the eternal WORD of the Father, one day wrote on the ground with His own hand! (Jn 8:6.) It is clear to the eyes of faith that any effort to make a graphological analysis here could only stammer before this writing that could not be classified in any known categories of writing which are necessarily limited. However, it is certainly closer to the hieratic writing of Vassula than to our own personalized handwritings which enter in well defined categories.

A Letter of the Lord to His Church

Therefore, if the Lord, when speaking with us, does not use the usual rapid, emotive and very moving handwriting of Vassula and instead prefers to use this hieratic and transcendent handwriting, He has His reasons. In all humility, and without exaggeration, it seems that I can say these things:

In other messages which have been entrusted to other privileged souls, the Lord is speaking to all souls of good will, at times to specific persons, at times to communities, or even to all the faithful (the shepherds and lambs). However, here He is speaking, first of all, to the shepherds, to those who are responsible for his Church, those whom the Apocalypse calls "The angel of the church of...." It is thus a LETTER TO HIS CHURCH, so very much divided for such a long time and still menaced by internal schisms, caused quite often by personal reasons rather than different liturgical traditions or different schools of theology. Moreover, who could claim, except for the God Man Himself, to sum up in a single spirituality, in a single theological vision, in a single sacred rite, the complete ineffable mystery of the Three Who are One!

Jesus, in this End of Times, in this Time of the Nations, wishes to make us come in direct contact with the fact that it is truly He who is speaking with us and writing to us. The secretary in this case is without importance and should vanish from our eyes. This is true to such an extent that even her personal handwriting, which reveals her deepest being, should vanish behind this handwriting which is apparently impersonal and artificial but is on the contrary transcendent. Just as the individual personality of the typist-secretary reflected in her handwriting disappears totally behind the printed letters of the typewriter.

Here, it is therefore the Lord who speaks, the Man-God. It is He who bursts through all the categories of character or graphological order in which one might enclose Him. He is the one who goes beyond all our psychological categories, all our schools of theology that we use to define Him. He is the One about Whom all our sacred rites and our diverse liturgical traditions try to stammer out the mystery without ever being able to exhaust it.

And He speaks to His Divided Church. He is writing a letter to it to announce that His Return is close and He invites us to a conversion of Our Hearts to His Heart in union with the Heart of His Mother by taking the path to Unity, especially in the united liturgical celebration of Easter. Then all mankind can believe that Jesus is Risen and is indeed, the Son of God and Savior of all. (Jn. 17:21-23)

In giving His writing this hieratic and sacred form so close to icons and evocative of Hebrew, the language of Revelation, does not the Lord perhaps wish to say something still more profound! Does He not wish to remind us that He is the Author of the Holy Scriptures that illumine all our human history and that as we arrive at the end of this Sacred History, He is intervening personally to open up the Book of the Apocalypse to reveal for us the mystery contained therein?

One cannot fail to be reminded of the passage in the Book of Revelation which is so evocative of the spiritual experience lived by Vassula: "I heard behind me a strong voice like a trumpet that said to me: 'What you see, WRITE IT IN A BOOK and send it to the seven Churches. I turned to see who the voice was that was speaking to me, and I saw in the midst of the seven Lampstands of gold (the seven Churches) someone who looked like a son of man who said to me: I am the First and the Last, He Who is LIVING... I was dead, and behold, I live forever and ever, holding the keys of death and the underworld...'"(Rev. 1:10).

"Yes, happy are those who listen to what the Spirit says to the Churches and who faithfully keep its contents, for the time is near"(Rev. 3:6).

I might add that normally Vassula, the secretary, out of respect for her Master, writes His Dictation on her knees. Might we not also receive (at least figuratively) on our knees, this letter of Our Lord to His Church, to the Seven Churches which we are?

Personal Reflection On A Visit

Priest-monk Joseph
Holy Transfiguration Monastery
Ukrainian Greek Catholic Church
Redwood Valley, California

Ever since a dark Judean cave opened itself to receive the Light of the World from the womb of the Virgin Mary, our Lord Jesus Christ has been in our midst calling us to the fullness of life in Him. He speaks to us through Holy Scripture, the ministry of His Church, and in sometimes quite extraordinary ways. Contemporary prophets and mystics are even now renewing Jesus' loving invitation to conversion and a deeper personal relationship with Him.

One of these chosen messengers is a woman named Vassula Ryden, whom the Lord recently sent to our monastery for a brief yet blessed visit. Vassula has spoken to large crowds in Los Angeles and Sacramento before coming here. She is Greek Orthodox, and was not practicing her faith when the Lord first manifested Himself to her. Since then He has completely changed her life, and now she lives for Jesus alone and for the mission He has given her.

It was not difficult to recognize in Vassula the evidence of one who abides in Christ and He in her. There was a peace and quiet confidence about her, and a joy that shone through as she spoke of Jesus. Her child-like intimacy with the Lord was manifest as she related to us her experiences of the tender ways that Jesus is present and attentive to her. She encouraged us to accept the truth that He is thus present to each one of us. Vassula witnessed to the love of God in a special way, for she was, in Fr. Abbot's words, "like the face of Jesus in our midst."

Vassula receives interior visions of Jesus and sometimes of Our Lady, and also locutions which she writes with the Lord's guidance. The messages are quite profound in their sim-

plicity, opening the reader to the spiritual riches of the Heart of Jesus, the Lover of Mankind. There are a number of themes which recur in the messages, such as the role of the Holy Spirit and the Blessed Mother in our lives, the precious gift of the Holy Eucharist, the holiness of God and the sorrowful condition of sinful humanity. The two most fundamental themes are, I believe, Jesus' desire for intimacy with us, and the need for the unity of the Churches. Thus we are called to respond wholeheartedly to the two-fold Great Commandment: love of God and love of neighbor.

A typical message of Jesus' everlasting love is the following: *"Come to Me as you are, do not fear Me, I am a loving God, full of mercy for the wretched ones; I am a God full of pity! Pray to Me, talk to Me, do not hesitate! I am eagerly waiting for you. My love for you all is <u>so Great</u> that I, who am the Holy of Holies, the Eternal One and Sovereign of all My creation, bend all the way down to you, to be able to reach you and heal your infirmities...remain in My love forever"* (11-21-88). This call to love is the essence of "true life in God," which is what the Lord asked Vassula to entitle the volumes of His messages.

As for the other main theme, Christian unity, another typical message: *"Unity shall come from above, for now as it is, you are divided altogether and do not live according to My Divine Image; you are not obeying My Law...your divisions will always remain; unless <u>I</u> put an end to it, it shall not be overcome; how could you believe that you can unite since <u>love is missing among you?</u>...My Kingdom shall come...you will all live in perfect unity under My Holy Name, and I, who am the Supreme Source of Life, shall regenerate you all into one Holy People"* (12-20-88). The Lord is grieved by the divisions and animosities among Christians, and deeply desires that His prayer for unity in John 17 be realized. If only we would begin to love and forgive and humbly seek reconciliation with God and each other!

Testimonies are many of people who have been converted by reading the messages and allowing grace into their hearts, and of people whose life in Christ has been nourished and deepened through meditation on these words of peace and love. It was inevitable, then, that Vassula would be attacked by the evil one and by people who misunderstand the divine invitation, or whose conception of what God can do and will do is far too limited. There are also critics who simply refuse to drop cherished prejudices or who fear the summons to break out of the illusory contentment of spiritual mediocrity. In all this the Lord has protected and encouraged Vassula, and her mission goes on, producing the fruit of the Spirit and drawing many hearts to true life in God.

Vassula would have us know how close Jesus is to us, how He listens to our every prayer and the sighs of our hearts. She told us how He "feels it" when we venerate His icons with love, and how He desires us to pray always and to do everything with Him, to the point of speaking in the plural: we, us. This is abiding in Christ and He in us; this is the unceasing "remembrance of God" to which the monastic Fathers are always calling us.

Now is the time to open our hearts to the mercy of Jesus, who is thirsting for our love and our generous response to His numerous gifts of grace. God forbid that we be among those who refuse this invitation to intimacy with Jesus and reconciliation with each other. The Lord does not keep silent but makes His voice heard when His people are in need or in danger, so "let anyone who can hear listen to what the Spirit is saying to the churches" (Rev. 2:9). What God conceals from the learned and the clever He reveals to the childlike, so let us come to Jesus with simplicity, openness and trust, that we might learn the art of loving—from Him who loved us first.

NOTE: In August, 1989, another seer, Myrna, an Eastern Catholic from Damascus, visited us. Both seers struck us with their common sense and orthodoxy, and especially by their self-effacing humility, their simple piety, and their total reference to God, whose mouthpieces they wished to be. Moreover, the monks' preparation by special prayer seemed to keep the evil one away. They are very allergic to fraud, unhealthy keenness for religious sensationalism, and lack of balanced judgment.

Holy Transfiguration Monastery belongs to one of the Byzantine Catholic Churhes, officially called the Ukrainian Greek Catholic Church. It is a place where the rich Byzantine tradition of contemplative monasticism is alive and life-giving, as they celebrate the full Divine Office, and keep the fasts. Theirs is a simple and joyful life of prayer, worship, work, study, and brotherly sharing, with an evangelical openness. Their goal is to create a true "family of Jesus" wherein the Gospel in its purity and fullness can be lived in practical ways. They live by the wisdom of the Fathers, and especially by the guidance of the Holy Spirit, who speaks even today to and through the Church. In all this they strive only to be faithful to the Lord, as children of the holy Mother of God, who sought to do His will alone. They are under the direction of Archimandrite Boniface, Abbot, in Redwood Valley, CA.

1

Arizona 9.4.92

Lord?

I Am; I give you My Peace; bless Me;

I bless You my King.

if anyone asks you for a message from Me
tell them that I have already poured
out My Heart on them; therefore, I have
spoken to them through you;* I have
poured on them the Treasures of My Sacred
Heart, this is My Message for all of them

ΙΧΘΥΣ ⽷

* That is: through this whole revelation.

2

Arizona 10.4.92

At the Church of Our Lady of Perpetual Help.

tell My children: bear fruit in holiness;
I have offered you My Heart, what will
you do with It?

Vassula, remember My Presence; My Presence
is Joy, Peace, Love and Holiness; ♡

17.4.92

So long as Your Breath blows on me
　　You will keep renewing me
　　　　　　and on my feet.
Breathe on me, so that I may not die Lord,
　Invade my soul with Your Light,
　　Yahweh my God
　　clothed in impressive Glory
may You be blessed.
　　　　　Amen

3

be in Peace; allow Me to lead you as I please,
I love you eternally, never doubt of My Love;
come, My child, together you and I, together in union with Me, together bonded
to My Cross, we will bring many souls
back to Me; do your best and I shall
do the rest; let Me use you for My
Glory, till the end; delight My Sacred
Heart and remain nothing; let your
heart be My Heaven; I shall continue pro-
viding your soul; praise Me often and
love Me, love this Heart of your Lord,

4

love this lacerated Heart of your Master;
desire Me and thirst for Me your King,
despise yourself so that you remain in My
Love and will not be deceived; do not
look to your left nor to your right, I
shall then perform even greater works through
you; you are pruned now and then but
I noticed how your weak nature dislikes it!
everything I do is done with wisdom from
Wisdom Herself, so My Vassula, allow Me
to prune you now and then, believe Me,
it is necessary for your growth; I have

5

chosen you for this mission to go out to
the nations and to bear fruit; I know
how frail you are and how much Satan
would like to see you annihilated from
the surface of the earth but I am by your
side; therefore, never complain, but accept
all of your trials graciously with love and
with great humility; the devil will be
disarmed and will flee with these virtues;
never give the devil a foothold ♡ no one
yet has grasped the breadth and the length
the height and the depth of My Love;

6

I want you entirely for Me, just for Me;
I am telling you this over and over again
from the very beginning when I called you;
I have espoused you to Me for My glorifica-
tion so that you work together with Me;
your mind now should be set on Me and
Me alone; pray all the time asking Me
for all the things you need; be obedient to
Love's desires so that everyone sees that
you are My disciple; I took you to Myself
to make you live a holy life under My
light; remember: you have one Master

7

and that is Me; you have one Father
and that is Me; you have one Spouse
and that is Me; you have one Love and
that is Me; I have taught you to live
by the Truth and in Love to enable you
to grow in Me;– once you were ignorant
of Me and enslaved to the world and to
creatures, but I, your Creator, have detached
you so that you love Me above everything
and above all; today I am asking you:
are you happy to be with Me in this way?

I am very happy Lord, You know it.

8

you have become an object of dread for
Satan, this is why you see now and feel
his fury, the more your fruit increased, the
more fires he built, accumulating falsehood
and fraud to accuse you; he wrestles with
the angel I have given you, he amasses
fraud against you, yet, in spite of all this,
do you still want to continue this Divine
Work with Me?

I, your slave out of love, shall serve Your
Greatness and Your Majesty till the end.
♡ My beloved one, I will continue then to

9

lead you with reins of Love ♡ come

☧ (Chi-Rho with A and Ω)

18. 4. 92

Fraud and oppression fill their mouth,
spite and iniquity are under their tongue;
there in the reeds they lie in ambush
to kill the innocent where no one can see.
     Ps. 10 : 7-8 (Samek) Pe

My poor and wretched instrument, grow in
My Love, I am He who adopts you, so be in
My Love and grow in My Love; you will
eat out of My Riches to reveal Me and glorify Me; Blessed of My Soul write:
     where there is mistrust and rational

10

thinking, there is also arguing and contention;
this sort of people intellectually are living in
darkness and are estranged from the Spirit's
Works; daughter, they have not yet perceived
My Beauty .... I have chosen your heart, My
child, to become My Tablet upon which I would
write My Love Song to all My children; I
made out of you a Hymn of Love; My
words are not printed only, My words on
you are alive and are Spirit; I have given
you sound teaching; do not worry about
those who come to you with unending

11

arguments and with a craze for questioning
everything and arguing about words; these
people are the prey to the Tempter and are
allowing the Tempter, by giving him a foothold, to get trapped into ambitions; lay
your hands upon these people and bless them:
"in the Name of the Father, and of the Son
and of the Holy Spirit"; you will honour
Me and glorify Me; ΙΧΘΥΣ ⋈▷

19. 4. 92

Cities are raised on a single Blessing from
Your Mouth, altars in ruin are rebuilt by
an instant look from You, and the dead come
to life with a single breath from You to

12

extol Your Holy Name, and all those whom You
covered with Your radiant dew made their
peace with You but everything is demolished
by the mouth of the wicked. Death does
not extol You, it is the living who praise
You day and night.
     you have said well, daughter, the prize of
the victory is with all of you,* double your
prayers, your sacrifices and your fasting,
treat your natural desires of the flesh hard,
treat your body hard and do not allow
it to comply with its cravings, make your
body obey you; be in a constant prayer to

* That is : Victory depends from us.

13

Me and in every course you take have Me in mind; I am your God; pray for your brothers and sisters who follow a false religion,* a false image of Myself; the devil has gone down to your generation in a rage; these sects were prophesied in the Scripture; Vassula, these false religions have spread in My Church*² like cancer in a body; these sects are the cancer of My Body; they may argue that true wisdom is to be found in them but Satan is trying to deceive if possible all the

* Sects like Jehova Witnesses, New Age, Moonies etc.
*² We are all the Lord's Church.

14

world, even the elect; the world's stubborn refusal to repent has led it to error; your generation knew Me, yet it refused to recognize Me; it preferred to follow in its obscured mind Satan's doctrines; I have offered My Peace but the world refused My Peace; the world instead exchanged My Glory for a lie, it exchanged My Perpetual Sacrifice for the disastrous abomination:

the spirit of rebellion

given by the Rebel; the world has exchanged My Divinity for a worthless imitation:

15

a mortal man, it has given up Divine Truth for a lie; but, it has been said,* that at the end of Time, Satan will set to work and that there will be all kinds of miracles and a great deal of a deceptive show of signs*² and portents and everything evil

that can deceive those who are bound for destruction because they would not grasp the love of the Truth which could have saved them; this is the reason why I am sending a power to delude them and make them

*¹ 2 Th. 2: 9-12   *² Satan, aping God, can give even the stigmatas, like he has given them to someone belonging to the sect of New Age.

16

believe what is untrue is to condemn all who refused to believe in the truth and chose wickedness instead; the power of the Rebel*¹ is such that he has without any fear appeared openly now to everyone; this is the one of which the prophet Ezekiel*² spoke of, the one swollen with pride, the one who claims to be God, the one who apes the Truth, the one who considers himself as My equal and says that he sits on My Throne. the Rebel is indeed the Enemy of My

* Freemasonry   *² Ez. 28: 1

17

Church, the Antichrist, the man who denies the Holy Trinity; have you not read: " the man who denies that Jesus is the Christ - he is a liar, he is Antichrist and he is denying the Father as well as the Son, because no one who has the Father can deny the Son, and to acknowledge the Son is to have the Father as well; " these doctrines of Satan teach you to believe in reincarnation, whereas there is no reincarnation; they keep up the outward appearance of religion but have rejected the

* 1 Jn: 2 : 22 - 23

18

inner power of it: the Holy Spirit and the Holy Communion, My child; Satan goes disguised as an angel of light to deceive many, and together with the Rebel* he will confer great honours on those who will acknowledge him, by giving them wide authority and by farming out the land at a price;*² but I tell you truly, that soon heaven will open and My Fire will come down on them and consume them,

Faithful and True, I Am,

* Freemasons   *² Dn 11: 39

19

Judge and Integrity,
I Am,
the Word of God,
I Am,
the King of kings and the Lord of lords,
I Am,
and I repeat to you My Promise:
I shall indeed be with you soon ♡

A ☧ Ω

20

20. 4. 92

Yahweh, I am Your slave, and I will offer You again today my will that You may do what Your Heart pleases with me. What a delight to be in Your Presence and to be allowed to walk with Your Majesty! What return can I make to You for all the blessings You poured on me? I have only to lift my eyes towards Heaven and You bend down to listen to me; and when I invoke Your Name, Your Majesty descends all the way from Your Throne, You who are Sovereign in the Heavens and on earth to be with me in my room and keep me company.

I come to you; misery attracts Me, poverty infatuates Me, so do not weary yourself with getting rich; set Me, your God, like a seal on your heart, and I shall continue, My beloved one, to demonstrate My sweetness towards

---

21

you;

My God is good to me, a stronghold when I am oppressed and calumniated, a stronghold when times are hard. My God is my protective Shield. Satan may sharpen his sword or may bend his bow and take aim on me, but, my God, my Abba ever so Tender, will be present and will make the devil flee.

give Me unbounded love, I am looking down from Heaven at you all, to see if a single one is seeking Me without self-interest; what joy and what happiness I receive every time I hear My Name extolled! but many have turned aside, many are tainted with sin; let My Heart rejoice in poverty, let My

---

22

Heart rejoice in a love without self-interests; give Me, daughter, as I have given you; do not appear to Me empty-handed;

My gifts are Yours, in fact all the gifts I have been given are Yours.

offer Me sacrifices; be generous, have I not been generous to you? give Me now, as I have given you, offer Me sacrifices to appease My justice; *¹ build what I have given you to construct ♡ *² O Vassula! offer Me everything to assuage My thirst! put your faith in

*¹ I hesitated. I did not know what did God exactly mean. *² I still did not understand.

23

Me; give those who wait for My Word My Hymn of Love, give, so that all the earth's inhabitants may hear My Merciful Cry; *I cannot ignore My children's supplication,

Lord, I beg You to guide my steps in the Truth and in the Light.

you will continue then to minister before Me and I shall open your mouth to fill it with My Words, to glorify Me ♡ and through you I shall produce a visible ♡ Image of Myself, I will touch the hearts of My people, and even people who never knew

* I finally understood that I have to continue more than ever to witness and make known God's Message.

24

Me will be blessing Me; despise yourself and I shall not reject you; I, Yahweh will save you; a✝w

20. 4. 92

Come back to us and dwell in the middle of our heart; let our heart be called: Faithful City and Your Holy Mountain.

little one I give you My Peace ♡ the advices and the supplications from your Holy Mother,* My agonies and cries from My Holy Cross to the world have remained stagnant; We have come to offer you all, Our Peace and prepare you for your journey to heaven, but Love has been rebuked and Peace

* I understood, our Holy Mother of Medjugorje

25

treacherously replaced by lethargy and a
spirit of wickedness; I went in all directions
seeking by what means I might awaken you
from your perpetual lethargy and return to
Me to live Holy, but I heard no sound
from you; what could I have done more
that I have not done? My friends, you
have not taken seriously Our Calls; I
descended to offer you My Heart; I have
inscribed you in the flesh of My Heart,
I have written you My Love Hymn to
all of you, — I visited you —

26

My Eyes stream with Tears and Our Two
Hearts are lacerated because you have not
persevered in the Path of Holiness, the world
made fun of Our Merciful Calls and no
one was really listening; I am your God
and Shield, full of Tenderness and I am
known to intervene quickly in times of tribulations, but you preferred to walk in the
shadow of darkness and in the valley of
death; My kindness has been repaid
with your wickedness arraigning Me for
trying to save you .... My Hymn of

27

Love* to you is constantly being ridiculed,
defamed and blasphemed for in your spirit
lies a spirit of darkness; you are harvesting
in the Deceiver's field to show the world
that My Holy Words are ignominious with
no substance*², but there too*³, you will be
wasting your breath when you will come to
Me for help in the days of purification,
you will call; but I shall not listen;

* That is: The Messages of 'True Life in God'.
*² Jesus is referring to these people who decided to
twist every word in these Messages to prove to the
world that these Messages are foul and not from God.
*³ Like in other times of persecution

28

men intent on silencing Me laying snares,
others are hatching treacherous plots all day
long, the wicked may hope to destroy
you, My child, you whom I have chosen,
treating you like the scum of the earth,
but I have sworn to maintain you on
your feet, I shall uphold you for My
purpose ..... I have told you, My child,
that your persecutors will be allowed to give
you impressive wounds, but they are for My
Glory and for your purification; your
life-span is nothing and you are but

29

a passing shadow on earth and your wounds and sufferings on earth are only a puff of wind compared to Mine; it is I, your Saviour who have kept your soul in My Arms and made your spirit live for Me alone, it is I, the Sublime Glory that put in your mouth a New Hymn of Love to sing it to the world and melt its hardened heart; look, you have given Me a drop or two of your life, and I, how much have I given you? I have given you to drink from the Eternal

30

Fountains of My Breast, I never failed you; in an arduous battle I won your heart, puny little creature, and made you Mine; I have treated you leniently and gently more than anyone else in spite of your childish inso-lence; I, your Creator, was charmed by your ineffable weakness and misery, and you, My creature, were left in awe by My perfect Beauty, and My dazzling Light; you are clay and out of the same clay I modelled and shaped others too ♡ I blew life into you and made out of each one of you a

31

portrait of My Image; I ask you to read: 'teach us to count how few days we have and so gain wisdom of heart,' (Ps. 90:12) your passage on earth is as I said a passing shadow, so cling to Me; you do not have to prove your innocence; * I your Creator, know you; My child whom I have chosen, do not be afraid, come to Me and I shall warm you; do not be afraid when you are glorifying Me; soon all that I foretold

* My accusers have met between them to judge and condemn me as not from God. They even took all the trouble to write a book against me. (5 people)

32

will take place and now when the former predictions will come true, many will shudder when they realize that :

The Lamb sitting on the Throne

of God

had truly sent among them a bearer, a bearer with good news and with a Hymn of Love in her mouth, to sing to all nations this New Hymn of the Most High, just as she had heard it from the Source of Sublime Love Himself, and that truly you were Mine from the beginning

33   23. 4. 92

My God, Rationalism, Modernism, the Sects
and Atheism have invaded Your Glory, they
have desecrated Your Holy Temple and defiled
Your Sacred Name.   They have reduced Your
Sanctuary to a pile of ruins. They have
left on their passage corpses of Your children
a prey for the vultures. How much longer
will You be away, Lord? For long?
                SHEPHERD !
where are You? Apostasy is devouring Your
sheep and Rationalism is battering Your sheep-
fold, in tenderness quickly intervene, we can
hardly be crushed lower; help us, God our
Saviour, for the honour of Your Holy Name.
We are Your people, are we not? The
flock that You pasture.
                Shepherd ?
how much longer, Shepherd ? Why hold back
Your steps? O pick your steps over these
endless ruins: Apostasy roared where Your
Heart used to be, determined to destroy all
that came out of Your Hand.
                My Shepherd

34

Loudly I cry to You, our strength is running
out, so tell me, how much longer have
we to wait? The time has come to have Mercy
on us, hear our sighs, and let our cry reach
You !

Soul ? I, your Shepherd have leaned down
from the heights of My Dwelling, have
looked down at earth from heaven, to
hear the sighing of My lambs, and to
rescue those doomed to die savagely; as
                My Word
has become a lamp to your feet a light
on your path, so will I spread My Word
in every nation to englobe you all

35

in My Transcendent Light, so that when
you walk, your going will be unhindered,
as you run you will not stumble; I
love those who love Me, those who seek Me
eagerly shall find Me! I have given you
My Heart to love: so love Me and I shall
do great things in you ♡ — little one,
My Return is closer than you think, I
am coming My Vassula to reign in every
heart; I have listened to you; do not
let your heart be troubled or afflicted, because nothing will come between you and Me;

36

I ask you, My beloved and My bride to
have constancy and faith so that you grow
in Me; I bless you, live in Me ♡

ΙΧΘΥΣ 🐟
                                1. 5. 92

My Lord Yahweh, my Beloved Father in
Heaven, Your Name is an oil poured out;
You have revealed Your Name to me by
coming forward to me and saving me; You
brought me up bringing me near You.
        Yahweh my God You have redeemed me.
Ah Vassula, though you were a dried up
driftwood ready to be thrown on the fire
to be burnt, I came hurrying to you
to save you; in the valley of Death

37

I have found you making Me plunge into mourning; My Cry turned the heavens in a state of alarm, the very memory of that sight still deeply grieves Me, such was the distress I endured; I was patient with you for many years; I called you many times then, but you would not listen; but, greatly loving, I did not make an end of you, I have shown you instead My Faithfulness in your wickedness; the pain and injuries you were giving My Son were devouring slowly My Mercy, so great was your

38

guilt and so many your sins that I was ready to avenge My Son's Wounds by striking you; ah Vassula, your Mother of Perpetual Help cried at My Feet, shedding Tears of Blood for you, yes, your Holy Mother favoured you and comforted Me .... My Heart was deeply moved and My anger was removed by Her Tears; the tempest that had risen in Me was silenced; I, Yahweh your Eternal Father, loved you with an everlasting love since that day, I created you and held you in My Hands; ah .... never

39

will I forget that day how small you were; I said : ' I will drive the Invader away from many souls through this small and delicate girl'; you and I then made a pact together, that you would work for Peace proclaiming My Love to resound to the ends of the earth, and that through your weakness I would rally those who would be on the point of perishing, I would make you fearless to threats and of invaders; and through you I would pursue and track down the renegades; then, in you I

40

would bring your generation to reconcile and unite; since I was to encroach on My Enemy's plans already, I had to bring your soul to consent with Me and strengthen you from the beginning; I said: sanctify yourself already and fast from your birth, this is what I desire: I shall not give you light at your birth;* for three days and for three

* When I was born my eyes were stuck together, they were shut. I opened my eyes only after 3 days. My mother filled with fright that I might be perhaps without eyes asked and prayed to our saint Paraskevi (a Greek saint for the eyes) for help and vowed to give me her name after Vassula. Paraskevi in Greek means : Friday.

41

nights you will remain in the dark, this
is how you will fast;" so this is why I
swore to widen once more the space in your
heart for My entry; and like a tempest I
came upon you to destroy everything that
rendered My Heart into a Wound; I blew
like one blows on the coal fire, this is the way
I blew in your soul to enliven the extinguishing
flame inside you; I said: " let your flame
now rise in your darkness to rejoice My Soul,
let your aridity turn like a watered garden,
like a spring of water"; and with

42

everlasting Tenderness I have pressed you on My
Heart, making you Mine again; I swore
to change your rebellious and unruly heart
into a resting place for Me; I made you
understand that I should be your only
God, your only Love, unrivalled and ir-
revocable; I then removed your veil to honour
My Name and declared openly to My Celestial
Hall, that I Myself will fight those
who will fight and persecute you, for now,
I, your Creator will be your Husband
and your only Refuge, I would be Me

43

who confides in you and you in Me; I
would make My words a fire in your mouth
to proclaim them to the ends of the earth;
all that you have learned you have learned
from Me; I Yahweh, your Eternal Father
embellished you, delicate little girl; I
stoop at this very moment, down to you
to lift your soul close against My Heart
My affliction My child, to watch My
children refusing My Love, My Peace and My
Graces are turning My Heart over inside Me;
I need souls to comfort Me, I need generous

44

souls to appease My burning wrath; be My
relief, be My Heaven; I Yahweh, love
you all; come, I will show My Glory through
your nothingness; for My Sake, put an end
to transgression, put a stop to rebellion;
you are all parcelled out and are constantly
failing your fruits to unite and live
holy; are not you and your brothers all
the same to Me? will not one of you
restore My Honour by restoring My tottering
House? will I be forced to draw My
sword on you? will you continue to

45

resist My Holy Spirit? will you continue recrucifying My Son? the Amen is asking each one of you to bless your enemies, to forgive them all and come and reconcile with Me, your God, so that you will be able to reconcile with your brothers, to make one single Body for My Glory, come and make Peace with Me; let everyone hear Me and understand by reading Me, how, I your Eternal Father am rendered everytime My Eyes watch from Heaven sights that lacerate My Heart, and how I can conquer the bitter

46

plague that invades more and more in each soul; I am the Amen and I can save you if you turn to Me; — Vassula, your race is not yet over, but I, Yahweh your Eternal Father am with you; be blessed for allowing Me to use your hand and your time; My Finger is on your heart so that you remember who fostered you. ♡

A𝚾Ω

47

My child, I give you My Peace ♡ write: 5. 5. 92

I am your King, and I am here to mark a Cross on the foreheads of all those who are sincere and who truly love Me; you are to say with Me the consecration of My Sacred Heart*¹ and while you are saying it, I will, with My Finger, be marking you with My Sign ♡ My Cross will be the Sign between you and Me; and I will love you with all My Heart, and I will guard you and fragrance you with My Fragrance ♡

*¹ Consecration dictated to me by the Sacred Heart on January 26, 1992

48

consecrate yourselves to My Sacred Heart and to the Immaculate Heart of your Blessed Mother, so that I may be able to make out of your hearts My Garden, My Resting Place and My Palace ♡   come back to Me with all your heart, do not come and stand before Me with a divided heart, come to Me and I shall leave a blessing on you while you pass Me by; I am your Hope so open your mouths to invoke Me with your heart and I shall fill your mouth so that you praise and honour Me; My sons, My daughters, be gentle

49

with each other, love one another as I love you so that in the Day of Judgement you may find favour before Me; I tell you, the days are coming when the unripe fruit will be of no use anymore, for your King who speaks to you today will reveal His Glory and you will see Him face to Face: so blessed are those who are ready to receive Me, they shall be called heirs of the Most High ♡ be one; ecclesia shall revive! ΙΧΘΥΣ ⵊⵣ

Our Blessed Mother speaks.
Children of My Heart, you are in these days

50

watching the world tearing itself up, knocking itself down; the earth is overthrowing My children, destroying them and bringing disaster after disaster in many families; the foundations of the earth are rocking from the evil it produced; I tell you, so long as you continue to allow the Evil one to enslave you to Him many will be buried in the dust of sin; I ask you, and I implore you to bury all that is not holy; how long will you hesitate to set out to find Him who loves you most? your Husband and your Creator?

51

He who gave you your redemption and His Heritage, the Kingdom prepared for you since the foundation of the world calls you all day long; you can become the builders and the planters of this generation; you can become the menders of this earth; repay the earth's guilt by fasting, by sacrifice and by prayers from the heart; happy the peacemakers: they shall be called sons of God ♡ receive My blessings

6.5.92

"He has walled me in; I cannot escape; he has made my chains heavy." (Lm 3:7)
Compassionately, however You come to their room to pasture them. (Message for all the prisoners of the world.)

52

peace to you; it is I, the Lord, your Redeemer; do not be astonished, it is My Holy Spirit who dwells in each heart who speaks to you; My Love for you is beyond knowledge and not until you are in Heaven will you be able to understand its fulness ♡ I descend in these days of darkness from My Celestial Throne, all the way to you, to allow you to know, as well, what is happening and what I am doing; I am coming to reassure you all of My Promise, I come to reassure you, little children, of My Love and My

53

Faithfulness to all of you; My Return is very near; I tell you solemnly, whoever keeps My Word will never see death ♡ and you who hesitate, doubt no longer but believe; - 'if you had failed to understand the teachings of scripture 'do not let your hearts be troubled, come today and confide in Me, heart to heart; which father would hear his child's lament and not have every fibre of his heart broken? I am your Eternal Father, He who loves you with an Eternal Love, and like a father who invites his children to share and inherit

54

his property, so am I calling you to be heirs of My Kingdom; ah ... would that these words of Mine were inscribed on your heart and absorbed by you .... My little children, you heard Me say: I am going away but I shall indeed be with you soon; I tell you truly I am with you soon; I have said that there are many rooms in My Father's House; each one of you has a room, give your souls peace and rest, by filling in this room, fill them by making Peace with Me; today Satan is vomiting all his hatred on the earth;

55

he tears up and overthrows countries in his rage, he destroys and brings disaster after disaster, but with great power My Hand shall build up all that he has torn; everything I have written in My Hymn of Love to you is only a reminder of My Word, it is to refresh your memories and to tell you with My Heart in My Hand that I thirst for lack of love; I do not bear a grudge against anyone, you are all My seed and I, I am your Eternal Father and Companion; I know well what is in your mind, but I am not here to

56

accuse you for your deeds, I am here today to show you how Compassion and Tenderness were treated, in My Heart I still have the lance's blade and a Crown of Thorns surrounds My Heart, the pillars of the heavens tremble at this sight and all My angels cover their faces in agony, the very moon lacks brightness, your God is being recrucified hour after hour from men's wickedness and spite; a Path was traced out with My own Blood to redeem you, and if your feet have wandered from this Rightful Path, I tell you, I have come

57

all the way to you now, to take you by your hand and guide your steps back in this Rightful Path; offer Me your will, abandon yourselves to Me and allow Me to tear down the wall you have built across My Path which prevents you and Me from meeting ♡ My little friends, your Holy One still has many things to say to you but they would be too much for you now, I will only add one more thing: if I have come all the way to you in your cell, it is because of the greatness of the Love I have for you; <u>call Me</u> and I shall hear

58

you; I bless you leaving a Sigh of My Love on your forehead; IXΘΥΣ ⋺

15. 5. 92

It was You my Lord who gave me true education of many of Your Mysteries, since You Yourself fostered me and are my guide of Wisdom. Your Wisdom made me to be intimate with You. " Grant me to speak as You would wish and express thoughts worthy of Your gifts." (Ws. 7:15)

Yahweh love you; remain near Me, remain near Me and walk with your Father ♡ repeat after Me this prayer :

O Eternal Father

Author of the Love Hymn,

King from the beginning,

59

You rose, God, to say something

to all the inhabitants of the earth,

True to the greatness of Your Mercy

and of Your Name,

You rained upon us blessing upon blessing;

over the waves of the sea

and over the whole earth

Your fragrance travelled;

Mighty God,

there have never been such lovely things

before in our generation,

Author of the Love Hymn,

60

Your Works are superb ornamentation,

magnificent, adornment to delight

the eye and the heart;

I mean to praise You, Eternal Father,

all my life,

and sing to You my God

as long as I live;

- Amen -

and I tell you: spread My Love Hymn with Me, your hand in My Hand; little one, walk with Me, it pleases Me, I intend in the coming days to irrigate My flower beds;

61

wait My child and you shall see My Glory;
My Love Hymn will grow into a river and
this river will grow into a sea of Love;

"I shall make discipline shine out,

I shall then pour out teaching like

prophecy, as a legacy to all future

generations;" (Si. 24:32-33)

yes, this is what I say, I, the Creator of
the heavens and the earth; and know
that soon, My whole purpose will be fulfilled,
city* after city will be inhabited by Me

* That is: soul after soul.

62

and rebuilt*; I will raise your ruins and
reconstruct My altars*² one after the other;
the ban once lifted, then all mankind will
be consecrated to My Sacred Heart and the
Immaculate Heart of your Mother; ecclesia
shall revive; a𝄞ω

Detroit Mi. 28.5.92

Vassula, let no one take away the prize I
have given you, before you I Am; pray for
the proud that judge My Works*², they
have no love for Me in them;

* ¹ That is: converted. * ² The faithful who were persecuted
and wounded.
* ² see p. 63

63

*² (Jesus was referring to the opposition that came up
in Detroit. There was a certain small group of
people who accused me of being a 'new-ager',
belonging to the new-age sect. They went in
every one of my meetings to 'boycot' the meetings,
distributing to all the people flyers with an
article against me.)

daughter, honour Me by proclaiming My
Messages in all these assemblies; there is very
little time left, these are the last days of
My Mercy, so stay awake, stay vigilant,
do not allow Satan a foothold; do not
allow your spirit to judge prematurely;
rid yourselves of carping criticism so that
in the Day of Judgment you will not

64

be judged; I am the Light of the world,
be prepared for I may come into your house
any time now; down from the heavens, from
My royal Throne, I shall soon descend in
your dreadful night, little children, be at
Peace, I give you My Peace, be patient just
for a little while longer and continue to
glorify Me with your love, I love you all
with all My Heart I love you; you are all
My seed, I bless you leaving the Sigh of
My Love on your foreheads ♡

1

Detroit Mi. 29.5.92

Jesus?

I Am; open your heart and receive Me; tell My people that I shall come to them soon ♡ on that Day every inhabitant in this world will know that I Am who I Am; pray for those who dispute what you teach, pray and do not allow your hearts to condemn them; have faith in Me and trust Me; Love is near you; glorify Me by restoring peace where there is dissension, love where there is hatred; imitate Me your Lord in this age of darkness; embrace My

2

Cross; My Cross will lead you to sanctity and into your room in Heaven ♡ Love will embrace you, ΙΧΘΥΣ ><>

5. 6. 92

little one, single-minded, defend the Truth to death, continue to give yourself to Me, your God, and consecrate all your days and nights to prayer, sacrifice, penance, offer Me your will and the Enemy will have no chance to approach you; keep the sound teaching you have learned from Me and do not worry when your accusers

3

calumniate you; I call to unity from My Cross, so never lose confidence, for it is I, the Resurrected One who calls everyone; it is not you, it is I, the Christ and your Redeemer who calls his scattered sheep; Vassula be gentle and patient with your accusers for they know not what they are doing; by loving them as I love you, My child and by giving yourself up as a sacrifice, you will be pleasing to Me; through your sacrifice I will have My House restored and many souls brought back to Me ♡ you who

4

are less than the least of all My children, have been entrusted with My Cross of Unity; My Cross of Unity is heavy but you are to bear it with love and patience; be My Echo and proclaim to everyone the Infinite Riches of My Sacred Heart ♡ you are to proclaim that Unity will only be built on love and humility; remain loyal to Me, your Lord, and remember that My Father created you precisely for this purpose, to give glory to Us* ♡ so stand your ground

* The Holy Trinity

5

and do not sway with the tempests;
I am beside you; do not be afraid, the
Truth will speak up; yes, My loyal
helper, you will receive from My Spirit
all that I have to say; My words, My
child, will be like a lamp shining on
the sacred lamp-stand, they shall be
like a sword in your mouth; I shall
open your mouth to speak without fear;
take courage, My child, I Myself am taking
up your cause; listen, today your accusers
are covered with confusion, but you will

6

escape their sword, here.... this is your
Refuge; see? this is where you are... I
am your Strength, your Stronghold; although the scourge falls on your back incessantly, do not lose heart, remember how
I voluntarily gave My back for your salvation without complaint; it is you My
priest, that the world will reject because
you are attesting the truthfulness I have
given you ♡ you do not speak as for
yourself, no, the written words are My

* Jesus with both of His Hands showed me His Heart
that was like on fire but a golden flame.

7

Own, your Abba's: I live in you and you
in Me; you are My temple and I live in
you; and now that I have clothed you I
shall remind you once more: no servant
is greater than his Master; if the world
has not known Me who am Master and
God and My Own people did not accept
Me although I came in My domain,
would the world today recognize and accept
anyone sent by Me? never! I have
said these things to you, My child, to
remind you that if the world persecuted

8

Me they will persecute you too; if they
wounded Me, they will wound you too, if
they jeered and mocked their King, they
will mock and jeer all his household too
and if they crucified Me, their God, they
will drag you too to Calvary and have
you crucified ♡ Vassula, your race is not
finished ... offer Me your life like a
good soldier, since I have enlisted you
in this Holy Battle to fight against error
and to be a threat to Satan and all his
empire; do not be afraid of the sufferings

9

that are coming to you, be brave under
trials, be patient like I am patient; today
Satan is deceiving many of you, the man
of deception is among you, spreading his
errors to an ignorant and somnolent lot,
because they preferred their own pleasure to
Me their God; some keep up the outward
appearance of religion but have rejected the
inner power of it: My Holy Spirit; so
then, anybody who is My servant and
comes from My household, is certain to
be attacked, but, My loyal helper, soon

10

I will bring you safely home, in My
Heavenly Kingdom;   pray and sacrifice
pray and sacrifice; look at your wretchedness now and then, that you may not
fall into temptation; never feel satisfied
with yourself; look at your misery so that
it keeps you alert and awake, despise yourself and humble yourself so that I may
lift you always up to Me and perfect you;
Satan is powerful, yet not for long;
hope, My Vassula, praise Me and glorify Me;
it is I, Christ, speaking in you; ΙΧΘΥΣ ⳨

11
                                    10. 6. 92

peace be with you ♡ love loves you;
flower, listen and write: like a man
who invites his friends to share his meals,
I invite you today to pray, but also to
share with Me My sufferings, My joy, and
My desires ♡ you are waiting anxiously to
hear Me and listen in silence to what I
have to say, and ah! ... how I know,
how thirsty some of you are! in these
times, as never before, I reach down My
Hand from above, to save you from the
powers of evil who are prepared to blow

12

out the little light that is left in you
and force you to dwell in darkness; so
do not say: "there is no one to save me
and no one to befriend me," and that
help is denied you; invoke Me with your
heart and I will come flying to you ...
                I am your Friend ♡
I am Me who loves you most; I am the
All-Faithful; I have taught you not to
refuse a kindness to anyone who begs it, will
you refuse to pluck the thorns that pierce
My Heart? for this I need generous souls,

13

I need today more than ever victim souls; is there among you any sensitive soul left? who among you will set Me like a seal on his heart? whose love, among you, is stronger than Death? have you not yet understood how I am sick with love for you, generation? open to Me entirely your heart, My sister, My brother, My beloved ones, for My Mouth is dryer than parchment for lack of love; abandon yourselves to Me; why do you fear in surrendering? you will only be surrendering to your Holy One,

14

to the One you say you love; give Me your heart entirely and I will make a heaven out of it to Glorify Me, your King; consecrate yourselves to My Sacred Heart and glorify Me; you are all of My Household and I do not wish anyone to be lost; if you remain in Me you will live; continue, My little lambs, to make known to your brothers and your sisters the consecration to My Sacred Heart as well as the consecration to the Immaculate Heart of your Mother; I bless you all leaving the Sigh of My

15

Love on your foreheads ♡ ΙΧΘΥΣ ><>

(Message from Our Blessed Mother.)

beloved children, do whatever Jesus tells you; give thanks to His Name for His Faithful Love; lift up your heads towards God and you will grow radiant, My poor children, I look from above in your cities where there is no rest and where there are so many upheavals; I look, but I cannot find enough love nor generosity ♡ I need more prayers, more generosity and love to help you; I find so very few to support Me in My prayers ♡

16

renounce all your evil ways and live holy; I need your prayers like a thirsty soil needing rain, to help you and embellish you for My Son; there must be no further delay now; the Enemy is determined to kill mercilessly and without pity and continue to thrust people out of their own country; I have seen horrors from above and My Heart is broken within Me; but I can restore the lands and I can restore Peace among brothers only if you will be alert to My supplications of Prayers and My Calls to

17

sacrifice ♡ loss of children, widowhood, at once will come to an end; take this time Our Messages to heart; offer yourselves to God and He shall take you by the hand and form you; he will make out of you a reflexion of His Divine Image ♡ with Him you will learn that: suffering is divine, mortification appeasing in God's Eyes, obedience pleasing to Him; desire what is mostly rejected by this world:

His Cross,

I bless you all with My Maternal Love ♡

18

16. 6. 92

This morning I was tempted and had a small doubt that God was really speaking to me.

"Yahweh, let my words come to your ears, spare a thought for my sighs, listen to my cry for help, my King and my God." Ps. 5: 1-2

Nassula, I Yahweh love you, remember My child how distressed I was, when I was telling you then about My children abandoning Me? * ♡ Nassula, tell Me, where have you acquired this great stock of wisdom in Scriptures if it were not from Wisdom Herself who smiled on you and became

* Message not yet published dated 19. 9. 86 from the Eternal Father.

19

your personal Teacher? .... Nassula, I am your Abba, let Me tell you: in the beginning you lived for one purpose, you lived for yourself, you served your vanity; you believed then that you were vested in splendour and glory; but in reality you were quite naked; no one had come to tell you how naked you were until I, Myself, came to shine on you and in your darkness; only then, your eyes for the first time saw yourself in the Light of the Truth, you saw yourself as you

20

really are; if it were not for My Compassion a sword would have awaited you; however, I pitied you and in My Mercy, I breathed in your nostrils reviving you; I then restored your memory to our relationship ♡ I did great things to you:

I espoused you to Me and you became Mine * ♡

I then formed you to become a child after My own Heart who would carry My whole

* Allusion to Isaiah 54, 5. "For now your creator will be your husband, his name, Yahweh Sabaoth."

21

purpose: to bring back My people to the real faith based on Love and share the Cross of My Son, the Cross of Unity ♡ I have formed you to live not for yourself but to live for Me; I have taught you, My child, how much greater it is to serve My House than to serve your vanity ;

now, spend your life with Me, for this is the lot assigned to you in life and in this Era of Great Apostasy ; so whatever work I propose to you to do, do it wholeheartedly for one purpose, to glorify

22

Me; the world is somnolent and runs grave risks, since it does not know what is going to come to them; out of their sin their apostasy will bring death to them; no one can tell when My Day comes; this Hour will come suddenly upon them; today I have done great things to save you, I planted Vineyards everywhere, I made gardens and orchards out of deserts; I am a Father afflicted by untimely mourning, because I watch how more ready this world is to kill than to love; massive child - murdering

23

initiations erupt daily; everywhere My Eyes turn they see treachery, murders, corruption adultery, fraud, disorder in marriage, people who sneer at religion, pollution of souls, perjury, sins against all nature, how then am I to keep silent ? this is why Justice will overtake this lot ♡ here I am speaking openly like a ♡ Father, anxious but offended and afflicted, My Voice is groaning from the Heavens, hear Me : is there any upright man left among you? ... (Suddenly God's Eyes turned towards

24

me, He stopped abruptly His dictation.)
Vassula, go and do your other duties too, I am aware of your time and of your capacity; beloved of My Soul quench your thirst in Me, I Am a Living Fountain of Purity and I love you, come, We bless you, come.

17. 6. 92
(Continuation of the message of 16.6.92)
little one be with Me; are you ready ?

Yes Lord.

hear Me then : how long am I to be

* The Holy Trinity spoke.

25

offended while you will not listen, to cry
'repent!' in your ear, generation,
and you will not hear? but look I am
stirring up the dead, these worthless people,
whose behaviour was appalling and far
from sanctity; the world shall be filled
with My Knowledge and My Glory, for as
the waters swell the sea, My Spirit
too, like a tide shall come in and no one
will be able to stop My Spirit from flowing
in; Vassula, pray with Me,

            Lord, in Your Strength and

26

            in Your Wisdom You raised me,
      You fostered me; in Your Love
      You helped me, and I
      became Your bride; Lord,
      You confided Your
      Message to me;
            praised be the Lord;
            come Lord, maranatha! amen
and I tell you: I am on the Path of
Return; like a traveller who left, I,
Jesus am well on the road back to you;

My Lord, tell me all about it, it makes

27

me happy!

My child I have spoken once .... I will not

speak again. ♡

What do You mean My Lord?

My words are clear ....

I still do not know what You mean, Lord.

look, My child, your God is coming!

Love is coming, He is coming to live

among you ♡

Tell me more about it Lord! We all delight
to hear, Hope speaking where there is
despair; Love pronouncing where there is
hatred; Peace announcing where there are
wars and conflicts.

28

courage! do not be afraid or saddened,
for these few days left; trust wholeheartedly
in Me; be strong, stand firm, yes stand
firm and I shall make your voice carry
as far as the clouds proclaiming My
Message, approach Me, approach Me ....

            A ☧ Ω

                              17. 6. 92

Yahweh my God, You who are so tender
and so close to me hear the sufferings of
He who is the Delight of Your Soul:
Jesus Christ, Your Son; the Church's gate-
ways are all deserted, and her priests
groan for her desolation. The City once
thronged with the faithful sits in loneliness
as if suddenly widowed. Your temples* are

* We are the temples of God

29

perishing one after the other as they search
for food to keep life in them but what they
inhale instead of incense is Satan's smoke.
Where are the domains like a garden?
Where are the blossoming vines that gave out
once, their fragrance?
Why are Your altars broken? *

Peace My child, peace .... hear Me:

the Great Day is near you now, nearer
than you think ♡ altar, tell everyone
that I will show My Glory and display
My Holiness through and through; I will
pour out My Spirit without reserve on all

* The three questions concern the soul.
Domains vines, altars, are our soul.

30

mankind; your eyes have seen nothing
and your ears have heard nothing yet;
today your hearts are sick and your
eyes dim because you are living in darkness and desolation and the Enemy roams
to and fro in this desolation; I, the
Lord will multiply the visions on your
young people and many, many more of
your sons and daughters shall prophesy,
more than now; I will make up for
the years of your aridity that led you
to apostatize; I shall send My Spirit

31

without reserve to invade My domains and
with My Finger I will rebuild My broken
altars; and My vines with faded leaves
looking now like a garden without water,
I shall come to them to irrigate with My
Spirit, I will remove the thorns and
the brambles choking them, and My
vines will yield their fruit ♡ I will do
all these things to save you; I will display portents in heaven and on earth as
never before; I will increase the visions,
I will raise and increase prophets; I

32

then will send you My angels to guide you
and I the Holy One will live in your
midst ♡ My people are diseased through
their disloyalty, they refused the gifts of
My Spirit because they trusted in their
spirit, not Mine, making treaties with
their mind; but now the hour has come,
the hour of My Holy Spirit to glorify
My Son's Body; come, Vassula, I
want you zealous, I want you to love
Me; so My child, I will instil in you,
fervour and a few drops of My burning

33

Love to enliven you with My Flame;

18.6.92

Vassula, let Me sing the rest of My Love Hymn to you, let Me stretch My Love Hymn for the sake of those who were not ready to hear;

Yes Lord! come and melt our hearts, show us my King, my God, the Riches of Your Sacred Heart. Show us the Light in Your Face. Let us understand that You, my God, are looking down from heaven to see if a single one is left with faith, with love, and if a single one is seeking You. Blessed be Your Name, blessed be our Lord, our Redeemer, Emmanuel, for He has sung to us His Love Hymn, even as He proclaimed by the mouth of His prophets that He

34

would return, thus He prepares us now for this encounter. And You, Blessed Mother, You who gave us our Redeemer, once more You are with us preparing the way for the Lord and preparing us to meet Him. And the Lord out of His Infinite Mercy will visit us to give us light in our darkness and guide our feet into the way of Peace, Love and Unity.

"Glory to God in the highest heaven, and peace to men who enjoy His favour." (Lk. 2:14)

My Vassula, I shall come to a people who never gave a thought for Me, never a glance for what I have done to redeem them and I shall make the prophecies of Isaiah* come true: "I have been

* Is. 65:1

35

found by those who did not seek Me and have revealed Myself to those who did not consult Me;" and the valleys of death with its dead and its ashes will be consecrated to Our Two Hearts be in Peace; come and repeat after Me these words:
            Jesus be my support,
        without You I am nothing,
                without You
            my table is empty,
        without You I am defeated,

36

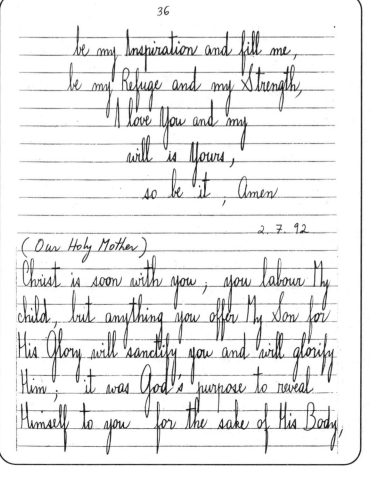

be my Inspiration and fill me,
    be my Refuge and my Strength,
        I love You and my
            will is Yours,
                so be it, Amen

2.7.92

(Our Holy Mother)

Christ is soon with you; you labour My child, but anything you offer My Son for His Glory will sanctify you and will glorify Him; it was God's purpose to reveal Himself to you for the sake of His Body,

37

the Church; daughter, remember, Jesus will never, _never_ fail you; remember how you entrusted Me with the Messages you are receiving? I, as your Mother, guard what you have given Me; and today like yesterday I will continue spreading quickly My Son's Messages; Satan may sound virulent and may appear as though he triumphs over every nation and that his victories are glorious, but, Vassula, soon I shall conquer him, for this is My battle; daughter, I shall comfort you and give you sufficient strength to

38

continue your mission ♡ (The Lord speaks now) please Me and announce My Words everywhere I send you, stand firm; lean on My Heart and feel loved; tell My children to consecrate themselves and their families to Our Two Hearts ♡ consecrate yourselves so that I mark you as Mine; hear Me, I tell you solemnly that there will come a time of distress like never before; the earth is already seeing the dawn of this time, stand firm and do not allow yourselves to be deceived; many are claiming that they

39

hear Me proclaiming messages, but I am not the Author of these messages nor your Mother either, I have already warned you of these times, I have many times warned you that in these times many false prophets will arise, to ruin your Master's Works with lies, the ears of those who hear will be alert, the heart of the hasty will be deceived ♡ (many will try to deceive you, Vassula, saying that I, Jesus am sending them to you, but they are false prophets;) remember many false Christs will rise, some will

40

produce great signs and impress even the elect ♡ there, I have warned you again; daughter? will you allow Me to continue this Work in you? pray so that you may not fall into temptation; I shall open the way for you, do not fear, My Love for you is Eternal ♡

Mexico 3. 7. 92

I am your Holy One coming down from Heaven to drench you all with the dew of My Love; oh that the heart of mankind turn from wickedness! I give you mighty

41

signs of My Love but who is there to
acknowledge My Love? Mexico! your King
is here to take you in His Arms;

I am here,

stooping down to you to whisper in your ear
the greatness of My Love ♡ have you not
understood that Our Two Hearts were the
Ones looking after you? Our Two Hearts are
here to settle in your homes and protect you
from the fierce anger of Satan ♡ today
I am calling your nation more than ever
to set your hearts for Me, your Lord,

42

every little one of you is so very precious to
Me; come, come and love Me; moisten My
parched lips with your love, I will heal
all the disloyalty in your nation and your
King will give you rest ♡ I bless each one
of you and tell you from the core of My
Heart:

Love loves you,

be one in My Love ♡

ΙΧΘΥΣ ⊱≺°)))⊱

Mazatlan - Mexico 7. 7. 92

We have failed to appreciate Your great Love
and we do not cease to defile Your Holy
Spirit, who now tries to adopt us and bring
us to the Truth based on Love. Apostasy

43

has intermarried with Rationalism that gave
birth to Atheism. We have failed You and
are continuing to fail You. Some are deliberately challenging Your Holiness. You
are speaking but who is listening? Grief wastes
away Your Eyes, yet all You receive is
contempt.

peace be with you ♡ pass on My Peace to My
dearest soul*; you must believe Me when I say
that My Holy Spirit in your generation's
great apostasy is persecuted like never before;
He has become the stumbling block of your
era. I have said, My little children, that
they will expel you from your Father's House

* Father Masi of Mazatlan, Mexico.

44

and condemn you thinking they are doing
a holy duty to Me! do not let your
little hearts be troubled, My beloved ones;
I, your Redeemer am before you; today, I
speak for the sake of all those who are
wounded; I give you My Peace, let this
Peace envelop you, do not fear and do not
say, "what am I to do Lord?" I tell you:
pray without ceasing to sanctify your own
soul and those of others; pray with your
heart and make the demon flee; be
united to Me and no one and nothing

45

will come between you and Me; the time has come when you should not hesitate anymore; spread vineyards wherever you can; do not fear of the tempests that arise now and then; My Sacred Heart is your Refuge, so come and consecrate yourselves and your families to Me and to the Immaculate Heart of your Mother; I Jesus intend to remain in your country and sanctify it, for this I ask you to consecrate your country to Our Two Hearts; I bless you all out of the depths of My Heart; IXΘΥΣ ⹋

46

8. 7. 92

" There was a vine: You uprooted it from Egypt; to plant it, You cleared a space where it could grow, it took root and filled the whole country. Your Message covered the mountains with its shade, You cedars with its branches, its tendrils extended to the sea, its offshoots all the way to the river. Please, God, look down from heaven, look at this vine, visit it, protect what Your Own Hand has planted. " (Ps. 80: 8-11)(Ps. 80: 14-15)

Lord?

I Am; little one lean on Me; Vassula of My Sacred Heart, rejoice! your King has come all the way to your doorstep and into your room; your King has stooped down from above to reach you, step by

47

step I have taught you, I am your Educator, little by little I have drawn you away from the world to plunge you into My Heart; I have revealed to you things beyond your knowledge and your capacity; believe, My sweet pupil, I Jesus love you; have My peace; we will work together; I and you will spread My Message; I shall send you to a few more nations, then when I feel you have accomplished your mission you shall return to Me; I, Myself, shall come and fetch you; α✝ω

48

Villeneuve, Switzerland 10. 7. 92

" There in front of the throne they were singing a new hymn in the presence of the four animals and the elders, a hymn that could only be learnt by the hundred and forty-four thousand who had been redeemed by the world. " (Ap. 14: 3.)

Lord?

I Am; I am speaking, so do not doubt, Vassula of My Sacred Heart, allow Me to write a few lines for this afternoon; dearest friends, I have come all the way from heaven to sing to you My New Hymn of Love, and remind you all of My faithful Love;

I am your best friend,

49

your dearest Holy Companion; all along I have been by your side, and although I have been many times ignored I remained with you to make you feel My Presence; every time you were about to rebel against Me, I, the Lord, full of Compassion, grasped you by the right hand to draw you in My Heart and show you My Infinite Love; blessed of My Soul! alone you are not, I am always with you to console you and guard you as one guards the pupil of his eye ♡ do not say:

50

"there is darkness all round me," I am near you to lead you out of this darkness; you need only to say: "come Lord!" and I shall be flying to you, My child; day and night I am waiting for your abandonment, do not delay; abandon yourselves entirely to Me so that you may be able to be in My Light ♡ if you love Me you will allow Me to ♡ do what I think best for you; do not fear, offer Me your heart and I shall place it into My Sacred Heart to consume it; if you love

51

Me as you say, you will sing to the nations My new Hymn of Love, to glorify Me and raise a new life for each soul; My Heart to you I have offered, will you offer Me yours in turn? Love is by your side and with the Sigh of My Love on your foreheads I bless you and your families; be one; IXΘΥΣ ⟨◝𓆟

(Our Blessed Mother.)

I am by your side to console you, but I too, who am your Mother need your consolation for great is the anxiety of My

52

Heart; many of My children are rebelling against the Most High; I need your prayers, offer Me your prayers for My intentions; Vassula, tell them to live as children of God ♡

14. 7. 92

"Lord, the first time I was persecuted I could not even present my defence;" there was not a single witness to support me. Every one of them deserted me —. But You Lord stood by me and gave me strength, so that through me the whole Message might be proclaimed for all the nations to hear; and so I was rescued from the lion's mouth. The Lord will rescue me from all evil attempts on me, "and oh are they many!" You will in the end bring me safely to Your Kingdom. To You be glory for ever and ever. Amen.

(2 Tm 4:16-18)

53

My Vassula, lead a life in peace, love Me and propound My Peace everywhere I am sending you; have you not yet understood My Power? so what is there to fear? I have put My Finger to your lips; you are not completely conscious of it, yet I tell you, My Finger is on your lips to pronounce all that I Myself have given you; no, you will not get by unscathed, but I have enough Power to cure you and heal your wounds. My Cup tastes bitter yet out of Love I invited you to share it with

54

Me; if I were not standing by your side, you would have been torn to pieces, so do not worry, no one can snatch you from Me ♡ hear My advice: do not get worn out; zeal for My House devours you and I am happy for your enthusiasm to glorify Me; nevertheless, the Bridegroom says to His bride: prophecy in peace and allow My Holy Spirit to be your Guide; My Holy Spirit will not saddle you with weights beyond your strength; therefore, do not prolong the requests and the

55

meetings, My Spirit will direct you so that you may give them sufficient; only the essential should be done; serve in humility, preach and teach all that I have given you; in this way you will glorify Me; take care about what you teach; repeat only the words I Myself have given you; do not add nor substract; be dedicated to Me; I am reminding you of these things so as to proclaim in perfection My Knowledge ♡ I want you to be My Echo so that those who are listening may

56

recognize My Voice; be careful always to choose the right course; Vassula, My Bride, the race is not yet over; do everything though in peace; I want My bride near Me, under My dictation, now and then, work in harmony with Me ♡ I am sending you to reap a harvest I Myself worked for, therefore, remember, console Me, desire Me, thirst for Me in My stillness, and allow your Saviour to rest in you; I Jesus bless you, ΙΧΘΥΣ ⛨

57
20.7.92

My flower, I Jesus bless you and give you My Peace ♡ I have been asking you all from the beginning to lead a holy life since I am holy; I have been asking you, dearest ones, to change your lives so that you inherit My Kingdom; when My angels who had been given supreme authority rebelled against Me and destruction took the best out of them, My Justice did not spare them, they were thrown down to the underworld to wait for the day of Judgement; they too will be judged before

58

the very eyes of everyone; and ah!.... what a terrible sight that will be! I will judge everyone according to what he has done and not done; in front of My Throne everyone will stand in silence and in awe for the Day of this final Judgement will be so dreadful that it will make everyone tremble with fright in front of the Supreme Judge that I Am; you will all see a huge number of fallen angels who were driven out of heaven and fought in bitterness and spite Michael the archangel and

59

his angels; yes, your eyes will see My Rivals, the 'Rivals of the Holy One', of the Anointed One; you will all see those fallen angels, adepts of Lucifer, the primeval serpent who tried to lead My sons and My daughters all astray ♡ you will see multitudes of those who defiled My Name and transgressed My Law, those who refused to be reared and fostered by My Holiness and preferred to be labelled on their forehead by the Deceiver; ......*

* I was here given a vision of this multitude of fallen angels, standing in front of God's Throne, in the Day of Judgement. It was awesome, and sad.

60

yes, Vassula, a harsh vision has been shown you; I tell you: I will soon come with My saints to pronounce judgement on the world and to sentence the guilty; today My Grace is being revealed to all mankind to renew you all with My Holy Spirit before My Day and remind you of My Law ♡ I will in that Day repay everyone according to what he deserves; I have said that I will severely punish anyone who insults the Spirit of Grace and treats My Spirit as foolish; that is why you should stay

61

awake; today more than ever before, I am asking you all to consecrate yourselves, your families and your nations to Our Two Hearts; allow Me to seal your forehead with the seal of My Holy Spirit; the Time of sorting has come, the time of reckoning is here; I said to everyone that I shall come as a thief upon you, when I return no one will be suspecting anything; then, of two men one will be taken, one left, of two women one will be taken, one left, the Harvest is almost ready to be reaped

62

and countless corpses will be left when I say: "I Am here!"

then I will say to My angel*: "the hour has come to sort out and pull out all who are not Mine, sort out from those who acknowledged Me, all those who have not willed to comply with My Law, sort out from those who allowed and welcomed My Holy Spirit to be their Guide and their Torch, all those who rebelled in their apostasy

* Allusion to the parable of the darnel. Mt 13:24-30

63

against Me*, sort out from those who are branded on the forehead with the Lamb's Seal, all those with the name of the beast or with the number 666;" the Time is here and I Myself am branding My people with My Name and My Father's Name ♡ Vassula, I did not open the floodgates of heaven to pour out My blessings in abundance for you alone, but My blessings are being poured upon all mankind now,

* This passage confirms St Paul's prophecy in 2 Th.2 1-12. The 2 foretelling signs of the end of times: The Great Revolt (Apostasy) and the Rebel (spirit of Rebellion.)

64

before My Great Return; you are, as I have been saying, living in a time of great mercy and grace, but the Day is coming now, burning like a furnace; and all those who have not been sealed with My Name on their forehead will be like stubble in this Day; I am revealing to you what is to come before I break the sixth seal*; come and consecrate yourselves to My Sacred Heart and to the Immaculate Heart of your Mother; as I have

Ap. 6: 12 -17

1

said, you are living in a period of Grace and Mercy; daughter, just as you changed from being disobedient to Me and have reconciled making peace with Me and enjoying now mercy, so will it be for those who are still rebelling against Me ♡ I will show My Infinite Love and Mercy to all mankind before I send My four angels at the four corners of the earth *   whose duty it is to devastate land and sea; I have ordered these angels to

* Ap. 7: 1

2

wait before they do any damage on land or at sea or to the trees until I have branded My Seal on the foreheads of those who have complied with My Law,* of those who benefited from My Graces and of My Mercy, to these I say : serve and do not wait to be served so that My Father in heaven allots you a place in His Tent ; by being faithful to Me you will undergo great persecutions , but have I not promised you white robes in heaven?

* Ap. 7: 2-3

3

have I not promised you that you will no longer be hungry or thirsty *? so do not fear when the tempests rise against you, Scriptures are being accomplished;

happy are you who die in Me the Lord! I shall indeed reward you My child, love is near you and ♡ My Spirit upon you; Hope My child is found in My Sacred Heart; Love My own is given to you freely, and Faith is a blessing from Me ♡ My Spirit

* Allusion to Ap. 7: 9-17

4

rejoices in your nothingness and My Soul delights in your frailty; I have raised you to console Me and delight Me; I have chosen you by grace to quench My thirst of Love; nothing to do with your merits since you have none ♡ are you ready, My child, to please your Saviour?

Yes Lord, I want to please you!

at any cost?

At any cost. All that I have as good is Yours. You are my ever Faithful God, the Holy One.

♡ I will lead you with a sensitive

5

hand and I will breathe over you to
spread My sweet smell around; be attentive
when I speak, My pupil, I have pushed
back a legion of demons who were heading
to plunder My property*;

Praised be Jesus!

come, daughter, we shall work; be
united with Us* ♡   we, us?

Yes!

21. 7. 92

Lord?

I Am; I give you My Peace and I bless you;

* me
* Jesus and our Holy Mother

6

flower, let us work. write:

"I tell you solemnly, I am giving the
world many signs but are they ready to
recognize My heavenly signs? many today
only speak about what they have seen,
but yet reject the evidence of My Holy
Spirit so manifest now; similarly, My
Holy Spirit will direct you as I have directed My disciples, overshadowing you all
with My compassionate Love; I will show
everyone that My Name, Jesus, means
He-Who-Saves; daughter, turn your

7

gaze on Me, and flourish, I am all
Bountiful; I invested you with My Knowledge and I have entrusted you with My
Interests; your Maker, has encircled you with
His Powerful Arms, so do not fear, I will
hurl down your enemies who in reality are
My enemies; your Holy Mother is your Defence; I the Lord shall make you strong to
carry My Message to the four corners of the
earth; night and day I watch over you,
so do not trouble your little heart, I
shall from today open more gates for you:

8

from today, priests, bishops and cardinals
will begin to open their ears and hear
My Voice ♡ they will begin to listen and
with a shower of graces poured on
them coming from My Infinite Mercy they
will begin to understand, and from their
eyes the scales encrusted by the dust of
Apostasy will fall and they will once
more begin to see the Splendour of My
Holy Spirit, they will perceive the
Fathomless Riches of My Sacred Heart, these
Riches reserved for your times; daughter,

9

consider yourself as a baby just weaned
from your Maker, remain small so that I
may easily lift you to My Breast and press
you on My cheek ♡ all wisdom from men
will decay, and the shrewdness of your generation shall be shrouded ♡ My Heart is
with you; daughter, you will continue
witnessing and being My Echo to this apostatized generation who are on the point of
collapse, you will be My ambassador for
My Affairs; I will, My child, carry you
on My Shoulders in the heart of a

10

nation who preferred to trust in wile and
guile than in the Breath of My Holy
Spirit; I will send you now to these who
have taken Me the Holy One out of their
sight; I will bring them a conversion and
a salvation such as was never heard of before
nor seen before; I will rescue this nation,
spare it and save it; in that day the song
they shall sing to Me will be like that on a
wedding night; I will send you to them* as a

* I immediately realized then that Christ meant
Russia. I was invited to go as a pilgrim.

11

- pilgrim ♡ " I will make the blind walk
along the road and lead them
along paths; I will turn darkness
into light before them and rocky
places into level tracks; these
    things I will do, and not leave
        them undone; (Is. 42 : 16)
I will come to save them;

A ☧ Ω

12

22. 7. 92

Lord, so long as we remain unreconciled we
continue to desecrate Your Holy Church, and
slowly but steadily continue to reduce our souls
to a pile of ruins. Are we truly seeking
You when we talk about UNITY? When
are You going to intervene and bring us back
to our senses to seek You earnestly? Are
we using our tongues to lie outright to You
pretending only we want to UNITE? How long
will we defy You and You will not intervene? We are repeatedly challenging You,
when are You going to challenge us?

pupil, repeat after Me this prayer :

    God, You who are full of Compassion,
let Your Face smile on us to unite us,
        look down from heaven,
            look at our division

13

that reigns now in Your Church,
Your lambs My Shepherd
are perishing in great numbers as
they search to pasture to
keep life in them;
listen to the groans of the Church;
this great Apostasy predicted is
robbing You of Your children,
bring to Your Church this
Day of Glory You once foretold
so that we may all be one,
Lord, do not remain silent

14

and do not delay any more,
come! come, bring to us the
Day once foretold, make everyone
hear Your Majestic Voice;
You are known to be Gracious
My God,
give me a Hearing and answer me .....
I give You thanks
for I know that You have heard me;
Amen
yes My Vassula, trust Me wholeheartedly,
put all your faith in Me, I shall never

15

fail you .... pronounce what you have to
pronounce!

Lord, where else could I put my faith and
my trust? You are the Holy One who
decides, You are Omnipotent so where
else would I go?

yet you are free to choose, even if you turn
to be unfaithful, I am always faithful, come,
write: I reprove the man who behaves
like a stranger to Me, I will set My Throne
in your hearts to honour My Holy Name
and I will shine My Magnificence in your

* Jesus looked at me gravely and said what followed.

16

little hearts; the time is almost up now,
I am coming to your help, I am coming
to your oppressed, by the road that I
came on I will return; I will enter My
City in Glory, I am coming, therefore, be
ready to welcome Me; O children! I am
calling you! My cries go out to all of you
and the foundations of the earth are
shaken from My Calls, how long do you
intend to sleep? when are you going to
rise from your lethargy and apathy?
disaster is at your very doors and will

17

overtake you in your sleep, suddenly, ir-
retrievably and you will still remain unaware?
but look, look Who is leaning all the way
to you, knocking at the very doors of your
heart; open to Me, My own, for My
Sacred Heart is lacerated for lack of love,
My Lips parched and with blisters for lack
of Love; open to your Holy One and console
Him as He will console you; I am at
your doors, do not refuse to accept Me ....
if you allow Me to enter your heart I
shall make a fountain spring inside you

18

because your soul would have acknowledged
Me as your Saviour; I will water your
so pitiable desolation and like a branch of
the Vine you will flourish and bear fruit;
come, daughter, I Jesus bless you for allowing Me to use your hand ♡ ΙΧΘΥΣ ⤳
                                                    23.7.92
Jesus?
I Am; love Me more, Vassula, are you
prepared? the Spouse then will continue
engraving in you His Work; you and I
are united in My Love, are you aware of

19

this?

    Your Breath blows on me telling me that I am
    counted as one of Your children, although my
    spirit still weak and uncomprehending remains
    perplexed at Your choice.

creature, your Creator is with you incessantly,
do not reach out for anything else but Me, I
am with you ♡   creature? your whole life
should revolve around Me, your life is in
My Hands and you are nothing but a speck
of dust; desire Me; today I made you
taste the sweetness of My Love and the
warmth of My Heart ♡ dearest soul, enter

20

into this Heart that loves you and R-E-M-A-I-N
there
♡   27.7.92
Vassula, My wretched bride, I had foreseen
all your failures and your weaknesses well
before you were born; I knew all along that
the one I had set My Mind on to cast out
in the corruption of the world to be My
Net, would wriggle and twist in My Hands,
I knew how the devil would place crafty
traps to trap she whom My Heart loves,
therefore, do not be astonished and do not

21

think that I am astonished either .... do you still want to continue bearing My Cross I so lovingly offered you?

Yes, I do. Do not hide Your Face from me nor Your Cross. Your Holy Face looking on me will give me the strength I need to carry Your Cross. This is all I need. I do not deserve that the King of kings so lovingly looks down at me from heaven!

Vassula, do not make Me change My Mind about your singleness of heart,* for carrying out the task I so favourably offered you, your spirit ought to be <u>united</u> with My

* This was a reproach from Jesus.

22

Spirit, your heart with My Heart and in this perfect union you will be able to be My Echo ♡ look! courage daughter! your Loved One is coming soon, to end up the sorrows and laments of this earth; listen, daughter, have* I deprived you of anything?

No, Lord, You have done only the opposite:
You filled my mouth
with Celestial Manna,
You nourished my soul,
You have done great things for me.

Yes! I have offered you a full table; I have offered you My House, My Heart and Myself; I have offered you to live with Me, in

23

My Light, I have offered you from the Palm of My Hand My Celestial Manna; I have offered you while crossing this desert part of My Cloak; <u>to keep you alive I have offered you to eat My Body and drink My Blood;</u> I have accustomed your steps to walk in My Steps; I have instituted in you My favours and the Riches of My Sacred Heart; I have held back legions of demons who were ready to tear you apart; like a Warrior I fought and defended your cause from the Deceiver; I have poured on you

24

and on your household My blessings; I have restored your house* from ruin and death; I have so lovingly pressed your lips on My Wounds and shared My Cup with you; and like a Spouse offering His matrimonial bed I have offered you My Cross, My Thorned Crown and My Nails to sanctify you; what more could I have done to you that I have not done? .... Vassiliki,*2 do not give in to the promptings of your nature lest you

* That is: "restored your soul"
* Jesus gravely called out my official name of birth.

25

lose your fruits and are left like a withered tree ♡ I have courted you, Vassiliki, with all My Soul and with all My Soul I intend to keep you forever Mine, yet I will from now on demand much more from you than before; if you do not stand according to the demands of My Sacred Heart you will face double your crosses; remember, you owe your life to Me and your salvation too; keep your distance from the world that has got everything but Me; may the Strength you receive from Me open your mouth and

26

proclaim My marvels, may every race in the world hear My Message; I shall sow everywhere and in each country, I shall cultivate your deserts and the sound of My Footsteps will be heard by all the inhabitants of the earth, to the far ends of the world; daughter, treat Me tenderly and I shall offer your soul delights and consolations to appease your thirst; get up at midnight now and then to praise Me and thank Me for the favours and the blessings I so lavishly poured on you; you are dear to Me, look on My

27

right side and see who is with Me ....
yes, your advocate and your Mother, guarding you from peril and from threats; like a lamp shining on the sacred lamp-stand;* She shows you the Way to Me ♡

On my way to Rhodos, Greece. 28.7.92

Lord, fortify Your city²* against siege, fortify Your sanctuary since I have to face a people who say to the seers; 'see no visions', to the prophets; ' do not prophesy the truth to us' and to Your predilected souls, ' you are damned: Have they not read, ' every kingdom divided against itself is heading for ruin; and no town no household divided against itself can stand.' (Mt 12: 25) And if it is through Satan

*¹ Si. (Ecc.) 26: 17   *² That is: fortify my soul.

28

thousands are being converted through Your Message True Life in God, a Message given by Your Spirit, a Message anointed from Your Mouth, through whom then do their holy priests convert? and so I tell you again and again, every one of men's sins and blasphemies will be forgiven, but blasphemy against My Spirit will not be forgiven, anyone speaking against My Holy Spirit and he will not be forgiven either in this world or in the next * ♡ and you, do not let your heart be troubled, I am with you, come My

* Mt 12: 31 - 32

29

Vassula, I and you, you and I together, see? have My Peace, we, us? come;

ΙΧΘΥΣ ><>

Rhodos Greece   2. 8. 92

Blessed be the Lord, my Rock, who trains me as His personal pupil.

Vassula, love Me and propound My Love; this is your Lord speaking, the One whom you say you love; I bless you My child ♡ ΙΧΘΥΣ ><>

6. 8. 92

Rhodos, Greece. (I have been asked to witness on the T.V.)

My friend, My little friend, do not hesitate

30

announce My Message and feel confident; I Am is with you; seek the Riches of My Sacred Heart and promulgate My fragrance, My Heart is an Abyss of Love, have My Peace and receive My Spirit, honour Me and glorify Me; ΙΧΘΥΣ ><>

9 - 8 - 92

Rhodos - Greece.

(After a rain of persecutions after I had spoken on the T.V., calumnies and blockages.)
Many conversions and repentances were made, during the program. But then a fire was lit by a monk, who combats the Lord's message).

31

Vassula, My Call has awakened many dead hearts; I shall speak for the sake of all those who are standing around you : remain in Me more than ever and do not fear; so much have I written to you about My Love; whoever keeps faithful to Me will not be uprooted by the tempests, but he who would leave the world to overcome him will lose My Heart ♡ the Spirit has anointed these Messages, ♡ the Spirit is Truth, therefore, no one will be able to obstruct the Truth; I have levelled a path for you, so pray that

32

you may proclaim My Message as clearly as you ought to ♡ take My Hand and walk with Me; dearest soul, I Am is your Holy Companion; all I have to say for now is: courage, be blessed, and be united; pray in your tribulations; all the saints are with you ♡ we, us? come; ΙΧΘΥΣ ><>

- Rhodos -   9. 8. 92

O Lord! Hear my prayer, listen to my cry of help, do not stay deaf to my crying. (Ps. 39: 12)

Faith My child, have faith in Me and trust Me; sorrowful you must never be

33

when persecuted; how long will it take you
to understand Me? look, I Am is
leading you and I am known to have
overturned kings and whole kingdoms
when these became an obstacle for My
passage; I have exalted the lowly and
overpowered the haughty; come, do not
blame the proud, pray for them;

ΙΧΘΥΣ ⵥⵥ

— The oppositions in Rhodos 10. 8. 92
O Lord, why is there so much obstinacy?
O Lord, I am starting to learn that great
names do not give wisdom; there was a
time when I hoped for much from their
mouths when they proclaim the words: UNITY

34

and RECONCILIATION, but I do not even see the
dawn of it either....

peace be with you; the sound of your
bitterness did not escape Me; have I ever
told you I will abandon you?

No, Lord.

so why do you worry? I created you for
this mission; come, look at Me; you will
always have good things to eat with Me and
your table will always be full when you
are with Me; creature! I will lead you on
the way that you must go; retreat into

35

My Heart when you need to rest; do not
lose your courage, Wisdom will instruct
you; devote your time to Me and I will
use you for My designs; I will use your
mouth to be as sharp as a two-edged
sword when you pronounce My Words; I
intend to teach sound judgement to the
ignorant; if you allow Me to use you I
will carry out My Plan; until everything
has been performed and has been carried
out My fervent desire of unity and reconciliation among you all will not diminish;

36

I have put on paper through you how I
desire you to unite; from the very beginning I have spoken clearly; Vassula, My
child, have you not read, that even a
small amount of yeast is enough to leaven
all the dough? therefore, do not give Me
any premature judgement ♡

Rhodos - Greece - 20. 8. 92

dear and faithful child, while you are weak
I am King; here I am sending you back
to your own to remind them of My principles; some of you have become mild

37

and tepid for you have welcomed My words without trust when you gather together in My Name; woe to those who sell My Blood to honour their name! woe for those who are satisfied now and direct their lives by their natural inclinations and ignore My Spirit! woe to those who will become an obstacle to the door I Myself have thrown open to announce My Message; woe for those who believe they act wisely with the world, they are servants of the world, not Mine, they are slaves of the world and espoused

38

to hypocrisy, corruption and all that My Heart abhors; you say you suffer injustice for the sake of My Name, rejoice! for My Day will soon dawn upon all of you with fire; rejoice and be glad when people accuse you and disgrace you publicly exhibiting you as a spectacle of disgrace for My sake and My Message, all the greater will be your reward in heaven for having endured with love the insults of the world; pray so that your chains that still bind you to the world may be unbound by Me; pray

39

for those who cannot tell their right hand from their left hand; no one is worthy of My Call so do not blame the proud; grace now is upon you and Mercy is enveloping you, your King has offered you His Heart wholeheartedly but I have noticed that not everyone has offered Me their heart entirely, not everyone is willing to comply with My principles, no, not everyone has gone according to My Heart's desires, but has listened instead to their own voice, that which is their own law because of their

40

weak faith; to these I say: pray that you may not lapse from My favour, pray that you will do My Will, let My words spread now and do not be subject to your human thinking ♡ I have three more questions to ask: why have you reduced My Voice?
what have you done with the Messages I have chosen to be read?
where has the man once so eager to please Me gone?

Father! forgive them for they know

41

not what they are doing! .... My child
prophesy! let your mouth with My words
be like a sword .... serve Me, Love is near
you;

Lord, what if they do not do Your Will?
then I shall withdraw My Heart, My favours
and My graces but My Cross will remain;

(This message was given to those who laid
blocks on the passage our Lord had opened.
Temptations, fear, doubts led certain people not to
trust and rely on the plan God had prepared
for Rhodos. Jesus warned them.)

42

For the group of Rhodos   22.8.92

Lord?

I Am; all I ask from you is peace;
where there is dissension give peace and love;
where there is confusion ask for My Light;
ask! ask and I shall give! respect each
other and do not allow your hearts to harden;
do not give Satan a foothold; be calm and
offer Me your prayers; how many prayers
am I hearing? pray and fast so that the
evil one leaves; pray more; remain in Me;
like children depend on Me; pray, pray
with your heart ♡

43

My Ways are not your ways, so do not give
way to your own mind; little do you
know how I proceed; seed everywhere and
wherever you can; I know your capacity and
I know where I am sending you; blessed
are you who are calumniated and ridiculed
for My Sake, I tell you, you will not be
unheard when you cry out My Name; peace,
pray and lean on Me; ecclesia shall revive!

ΙΧΘΥΣ   ><>

23.8.92

(Locution very early that morning.) I heard Jesus
tell me after I had been praying to Him:
" I am happy that you are taking time

44

so early in the morning to talk to Me. Tell
them (the group of Rhodos) that My Heart
is an Abyss of Love. Tell them that
they should not put Me to the test anymore. " (And that they should read
1 Cor. 14: 26 - 32.)

Later on:

O Lord Jesus Christ, to Your most Sacred
Heart I confide this intention:
       Help us and shepherd us,
give us Your Peace, Son of the Eternal Father,
     lower us, so that Your Eyes, King of
            the Heavens, may look
            down from above,
     O Beloved Son of our Father,
do not allow multitudes to be crushed,
     men are dying of corruption,
speed Your Work O Holy One of the Father,
     and may Your Return be hastened;
You who are the Delight of the Father,
       do not allow the world anymore
            to defy the glorious Presence

45

of Your Holy Spirit.
My eyes are turned towards You O Lord,
and my heart takes its refuge
in Your Sacred Heart
to obtain Peace and Love,
do not leave me defenceless!
Amen.

I have made you fearless of men; this is My doing; in My Day I shall have an answer for those who taunt Me now; as for you My daughter, I find My delight in your nothingness;

the Son of your Father

tells you: I shall continue to spread out My Messages, those who oppose Me will run

46

into the Cornerstone and will be crushed

the Delight of the Father

tells you: I am doing a great Work that no man can stop, and as for those who charged on you bitter accusations I tell you, their hands will drop and their plans will not work out ♡ My Heart is consumed with longing for your love, generation and is ablaze like a burning Furnace; I love you all with all My Heart, with all My Heart I love you! behold, I will pour out My Love to you all to adorn your

47

wretchedness;

Lord, how is it the world has become so corrupt?

have you not read: where there is no guidance, a people falls;* the mouth of the perverse brings forth no wisdom, yet he who perverts will be found out; nothing remains hidden in My Eyes; but in these days of Mercy, My Hand is still stretched out for anyone who will cry out repentance, they shall be rescued; Love is near you My little loyal friend; the Amen blesses you, come

* Pr. 11:14

48

and worship Me;   I Am ♡

26.8.92
Greece - Island of Simi - Panormiti - (Panormiti' is St. Michael) (I went and stayed four days on this small island and at Panormiti. Only very few houses are there with a predominating Monsastery and Church of St. Michael. His icon is human size all covered in silver. It is a miraculous icon. I felt called there, so I went to pray and ask St. Michael for His intercession. Before leaving for Panormiti that morning at 8.00 AM Jesus came to me in a dream-vision. He did not allow me to look at Him. He wanted me only to feel Him. He stood at my right side and just then He put His left Arm around my shoulder. Immediately I felt God's warm consoling protection. My soul rejoiced! He allowed me to touch His left Hand which held me. I felt each of His Fingers. Then He allowed me to touch with my left hand His Heart, His Beard, then part of His Holy Face; every one of these seconds put my soul in an indescribable consolation, peace, joy and reassurance. He did not

49

need to talk. His Presence so close to me was
telling me everything.　I AM is with me.

(Later on that day.)

My Peace I give you; be patient as I am
patient; the Father loves you and has entrusted you with this mission; do not think that
I am not aware of its weight; I am your
Spouse who will provide you,* console you
and remain faithful to you; you are the
writing tablet of the Father and on this
tablet the Father's and My Hymn of Love

* Jesus reminded me of the vision, His Presence.

50

is being written; do not assume that the
Most High cannot find a way to carry
out His Plan among your people*; He will
come back to His Vineyard with Fire and
make an end of the tenants who have been
given freely His Vineyard and give it to
others because they have not kept It but
made a desolation out of It; I have been
trying through the years to warn them
by sending them My servants but they

* To face the Orthodox in Greece and talk about
Unity this summer was as if UNITY will never be.
I felt very discouraged. God made me the "go-
between," to bring everyone together. It is not easy.

51

killed each one of them;* today in truth I
tell you: 'the stone which the builders rejected
proved to be the keystone'*² today My Holy
Spirit of Grace is the cornerstone and anyone who falls on that stone will be dashed
to pieces; anyone it falls on will be crushed;
I have given you all a strong warning, do
not put Me to the test any more and
you daughter, do not be surprised at the
reluctance your people have, no prophet

* Here I understood that God had been sending
chosen souls with messages to them (the Greek
priests, monks) but their incredulity 'killed' the Spirit.
*² Ps 118:22

52

is ever accepted in his own country, were
that possible then they would not have
turned today into your enemy simply by
having been truthful to them; come, I
bless you and your companions; ΙΧΘΥΣ ⊂χ⊃

　　　　　　　Simi - Panormiti - 27.8.92

Nassula, listen to My Archangel whom you
came to visit:

' child of God, do not fear, stand firm
when they persecute you, you are not alone
give your True Shepherd all your problems
and He will guide and lead you;

53

and the Mighty One has His Hand on you; listen when He speaks for He has great plans on you; He is the living God and there is no one above Him; I shall help everyone who is willing to overcome the Evil One and in the Father through the Father I will undo the work of the devil; let anyone who wants to boast, boast of the Lord! praised be the Lord; remain in His Heart and remember, He has truly spoken to you ♡ God's Archangel Michael

54

7. 9. 92

Faithfulness is the essence of Your word, and Your word is integrity itself. Our life is in Your Hands, and yet our liberty is ours. It is Your Gift to us. But what have we done with our freedom? We used it to ensnare ourself and made out of it a destructive weapon for our soul. We need Your Holy Spirit to intervene, that ever-flowing Source of River water. Let it gush now on us.

Ah Vassula.... the paths of this generation will in the end be straightened and men will be taught faithfulness and integrity; just wait and you shall see.... as long as you live and there is breath in your body, I will shepherd you; I will keep instructing you in the fulness of My Wisdom;

55

I shall guard you against stumbling; I the Most High have favoured you, be happy soul be happy! listen now and understand: there is no poison worse for the soul than the poison of blasphemy to My Holy Spirit; anyone who blasphemes against My Holy Spirit will not be forgiven; so be on the watch that you may not find yourselves blaspheming against My Holy Spirit; that is why My Wisdom says to you; beware not to apostatize and reject My Holy Spirit of Truth who descends to you in these days

56

to revive your lethargy; in My days on earth they hated Me for no reason, yet on the Cross I asked the Heavenly Father to forgive them; today if the world rejects My Holy Spirit of Grace and mocks Him calling Him evil or foolish they will find themselves unrepentant when My Day comes, you who received a share of My Holy Spirit once, would fall from Grace and you shall not be renewed a second time, how would you since you would be unable to repent with your heart and I will be coming

57

and will still find you unrepentant, with your heart hard as stone, dry and without fruit ....* I will have to cut you and throw you to be burnt; therefore, in all truth, I tell you, <u>open your hearts</u> and understand how My Holy Spirit blows any-where He pleases, and breathes freely in My envoys ♡ recognize them by their fruit and do not ♡ be slaves of your mind ♡ every soul should know how mockery, jealousy,

* Jesus suddenly stopped here then very gravely said the following words.

58

carping criticism, judgement and calumny, opposes the Holy Spirit of Truth; you should be awake and praying not to be put to the test; I say this to you today: if your lips should cause you to sin, fast then with your lips*¹ rather than have your lips condemn you and your soul burn with agony,*² you must love your neigh-bour as yourself; you will say now: but You have given us this command

*¹ Jesus means to give a vow of silence.
*² Jesus means in purgatory.

59

already; yes, I have, but have you followed it? pray and ask for My Holy Spirit to come and rest on you! Vassula, let My Holy Name be always on your lips and in your heart; I am your Educator, and My favour is upon you; console Me and let your heart be My heaven; realize who I am ♡ pray with joy and I shall court you; praise Me and I shall envelop you with My imperishable Light; bless Me and satisfy My Heart and I Myself shall come to you and carry you across My threshold

60

into My House; yes, just like a Bridegroom carrying his bride across the threshold, I too will come delicately with great tenderness and love and carry you to show you My Throne of Glory; I have sent you My Holy Spirit from above to rest on you and teach you what you have never heard of, to save you and millions of others; remain near Me, My sweet disciple, our journey is not yet over, we still have a mile to go to teach the rest of My children the Know-ledge of holy things; I shall deliver you

61

to many nations to honour My Holy Name
and on you will be written My Knowledge;
I shall grant you to speak as I would wish
you to speak ♡ let now your heart rejoice
and treasure what I have said to you,
never fail Me; love Me and absorb Me;
I am Love ♡ ΙΧΘΥΣ ⸺⊃°

9. 9. 92

(Our Holy Mother.)

peace be with you; tell My children of Russia
that I Myself will train them spiritually; I
am their Mother; I am the Woman of the
Apocalypse; Russia, My daughter, be patient

62

the smell of death will not spread any more,
indeed your sufferings are soon coming at an
end, for the Lord in His Mercy will lift
from you the shroud of death that had
enveloped you so many years; your eyes,
Russia, My daughter, are soon going to look
on your King, your Saviour in all His
Splendour, who is known by the Names:
Faithful and True; your King is on His way
of return; Russia, listen to Him:
* those who are far away will come and

* Our Lord now speaks.

63

repent; they will rebuild My Church and I
for My part will anoint each heart, and as
someone roused from his sleep, Russia, will
rouse quivering with impatience to be consumed
by Me; I will deliver you and place you
as head of many nations*; foreigners will
grow faint of heart upon seeing your beauty;
your right hand will be in My Hand;
I will lift you high above everyone else
and I will perform My pleasure in you;
your Maker with delight and great joy

* spiritually I think.

64

will display your beauty to His people*, to His
angels and to all His saints; and the heavens
will declare openly their joy; the vault of
heaven will proclaim My glory at the four
corners of the earth ♡ Russia .... you were
dead, and I had put sackcloth on to
manifest My grief and like a father mourning
his child, I went about dejected and sorrow-
ing; now I have selected you among many
nations to manifest My Glory through you;

* Jesus had a happy voice and His Face had a happiness. He appeared as a father lifting up in the air
his child.

1

soon, your Holy Mother will topple Satan's throne to the ground and crush the Serpent's head; loss of children and widowhood at once will end; the dragon will be handed over to his fate and the world will have a period of peace ♡ the Mother of all humanity will prevail in the end and I, the Lord your God will triumph in every nation, in every heart and in every race; a✝w

* This last passage means that all the peoples of the world would recognize Jesus as the Christ. The Lamb.
    Allusion to Ap. 6 : 15-16

2

9. 9. 92

My daughter, the world is offending Me daily, lacking reverence to My Holiness; they misuse the freedom I have given them by destroying themselves; this generation has become an unsightly blot in My Eyes; they repay evil with evil, this is why I shall not spare this generation; no one can say I have not warned them, no one can say I have not been patient; the earth soon will shake and with a roar the sky will vanish leaving everyone in total darkness and with great violence the elements of the

3

earth, the mountains and islands will catch fire and wear out; every blade of grass will burn and in front of Me you will stand, disarmed, generation; the power is in your mouth to cry out to Me and repent; but you prefer to be homeless and err in sin, you prefer to live in deserts,

    Lord, I feel Your Sacred
    Heart so grieved. You will tell me
    to feel sorry for my brothers and sisters
    instead. I do but I also feel sorrowful
    for Your sadness for Your Heart is lace-
    rated. With Your Grace my Lord You
    can turn anyone acceptable in Your Eyes.
    You can make us ready to do Your Will.
    I, who am as You said, the least of

4

least have been entrusted with this mission with
    Your Grace, why not others ? I have been
    given a free gift, Your Grace, why
    can't others receive it to ?

you are bold Nassula, to inquire My Wisdom*¹;

    Perhaps I am bold, but it is because I know
    how Your Heart feels. It does not please
    You either to punish us and abase us.

everything that comes from earth returns to
earth*²; the sins of your generation have
pierced all Eternity, they have pierced My
Heart; pray and intercede, My Nassula,

*¹ Majestially Jesus pronounced these words.
*² I understood that we are self-destructing
    ourselves by our apostasy.

5

that there will be still time to mark as many as I can with My Seal before My Day, for good and bad will suffer in these days ; A✗Ω

10.9.92

Lord, my God !

I Am ♡ little one, I am the Author of the Messages : True Life in God, they are My gift to you all ; they are to make you understand My Heart and how I stand by you always and everywhere ♡

11.9.92

peace be with you ; daughter, what I shall

6

ask from you today are the following :

- deny yourself longer from food ;

- rest when you must and do not save your rosary for midnight !

- go to confession more often ; do not say yes and then not do it ; it is better to say ' I will try to please you Lord '! your King is aware of your capacity, the depth of your wretchedness and your amazing weakness ; pupil, your Teacher will not deny you of His Light, He will give you enough Light to grow and follow

7

the footprints of your Teacher and what awaited the Teacher will await the pupil ; have I not said, " the disciple is not superior than his teacher, nor the slave to his master ; it is enough for the disciple that he should grow to be like his teacher and the slave like his master ; if they have called the master of the house Beelzebul, what will they not say of his household ? " (Mt. 10: 24, 25) if My own relatives believed I was out of My Mind,* what would you not hear then from only your friends ? come, embrace My

* Mk. 3:21

8

Cross and learn from your Master ; My Soul rejoices every time I hear you pray ♡

14.9.92

Jesus ?

I Am ; little do you know how much I prayed for you to the Father, let alone your Holy Mother ! My Eyes stream with Tears daily because of the crimes of this world .... My Eyes are worn out looking for generous souls ♡ My Heart is troubled and My whole being shudders with pain to the point that I refrain to look down on this generation's sins lest My

9

Cup brims over; I have made a new hymn of Love* to sing to you and reach each heart from the heavens to save you and remind you of My Eternal Love I have for each one of you; I have spoken from above, not to impose My rules on you, but propose to you an alliance of Peace and Love to lead you all under My Wings and unite you; I proposed to wed you .... but how many of you understood what I had been saying? have you really understood what the Spouse had offered you? explain then to

* These messages

10

Me why every time I speak of reconciliation you turn your eyes away from Me .... – I was a stranger and you did not welcome Me, I was at your door knocking and you did not hear Me; though I have spoken the Truth, your tongue never ceased to tell foul lies about Me, judging Me and condemning Me; I have come to teach you good sense and remind you of My Knowledge, leadership and service, but you mocked Me and jeered at Me; I visited you with love and tenderness with a yearning to unite you all in My Heart

11

and teach you all over again the rules of My primitive church, but you allowed your own rules to invade your spirit throwing Me out of your heart; you will ask: "when, have I done all these things to you Lord?" I tell you, you have done them already to Me; you judged Me prematurely and allowed your lips to condemn Me, for what you have done to My envoys you have done it to Me; you profaned their name, thinking you were doing Me a favour, but in reality you were profaning My Name; how can you

12

still say: "Your Word, My Lord, is a lamp to my feet, a light on my path", when you have not received My Word nor reconciled with your brother? with great Love and Tenderness Our Two Hearts in these last days have been out* teaching you all over again that prayer, love and humility are the KEYS to your salvation, but how many of you have really penetrated this Truth? your heart is the gateway through which I can enter to heal you and

* Allusion to Ap. 11

13

guide you in My Path; have you really treasured Our Words in your heart or are you still out for war? you cannot hide from Me nor can you say I have deprived you of the Truth; explain then to Me, if you claim you are in the Truth, your division ....

open your eyes My friend! open your heart, not your mind! I tell you again:

there is not a good man left, no, not one really, there is not one who understands since all of you are under sin's dominion, not one who looks for Me, all

14

have turned aside, tainted all alike and yet many of you claim to be in the light;

I tell you, so long as you remain divided you are still in the dark; so long as you rejoice in your division, you are still not knowing where you are going because it is too dark to see; I have come to you to offer you a free gift: the gift of My Love, but Love again was misunderstood, rejected and alien in your heart; in spite of all My pleas to reconcile you and unite you,

you go on sinning; how can I forgive

15

your sins when you are repeatedly repressing My Words? you hear My Voice but you no longer recognize It; unless you allow Me to uproot all that is not Me in your heart, you will never see how today My Holy Spirit seeks in you more than any time: reconciliation and unity;

I have shown you how to unite, unity will be in your heart, reconciliation will be in the heart and not by a signed treaty! how can any man claim he is just when your countries are at war

16

and aflame? learn, that My Sacred Heart seeks from you:

charity, generosity, prayer, and a spirit of reconciliation, and to love one another as I love you; will I hear from you your cry of surrender and of repentance?

☧

Messages for those working for these messages. 17. 9. 92

My child, trust Me; you are unable to lift your little finger on your own; all power comes from Me; reward Me now and offer

17

Me your will ♡ I am waiting ....
          MY WILL IS YOURS!
I Jesus tell you : you enjoy My favour, for
you are under My authority; tell all those
whom My Heart selected that I shall never
fail them; the Spouse will provide their
needs; let everyone see in them true witnesses,
let everyone know there is truth in them by
their way of sharing; I am sending them
out to face the world; they must abstain
from carping criticism, so that their tongue
does not kill them or divide them;

18

not one of them has earned this grace, I
Jesus, offered them freely the grace, so no one
should ask for money; the strong should
support the weak, the rich the needy; as
I have said, " there is more happiness in
giving than receiving" (Acts 20 : 35) I will
give you enough to cover your expenses so
do not ever put Me to the test;* be
united in Me and among you, never give
way to despair in your trials; do your

* Jesus means that no one should owe money to anybody
or to any place.

19

best and I will do the rest! courage,
pray so that you may not sink; reveal
the Riches of My Sacred Heart and My
Glory to the world; you want to be witnesses
of the Most High? die then to yourself;
you want to be one with Me? detach
yourself from the world; you want to
serve Love? follow My Footprints drenched
in My Sacrificial Blood*; remember one
last thing : to be set free from your
human inclinations and weaknesses, ask

* Here Jesus asks us for real sacrifice..

20

My Spirit to help you; ask! and it shall
be given to you; I am gentle and humble
of heart and I know everything in your
hearts, so ask My Spirit and My Spirit
will come to your help; the Spirit now asks
you to pray often this prayer :

          Jesus, neither death, nor life,
       no angel, no prince, nothing that
          exists, nothing still to come,
       not any power or height or depth,
          nor any created thing,
             will ever come to separate

21

me from You; I vow to
remain faithful to You,
this is my solemn vow;
help me keep this vow forever
and ever;   Amen

.... up daughter and thresh! let your thoughts be My Thoughts; abandon yourself to Me so that all you do will be done in My Spirit and according to My Mind

allow My Spirit to breathe freely in you and I will accomplish My Will in you; happy are you, My child, who meditate

22

and allow My Wisdom to be your personal Teacher! for She will reveal to you many more secrets ♡ receive and give, give!

25. 9. 92

Here I am, to pick up my steps over these endless ruins, with a load on my back.
I come to You for consolation, for relief, and now the strength in me trickles away, and I am gnawed by grief that never sleeps. With immense effort I cross the terrors of this endless Night, enfeebled by the cynicism of these false witnesses who plague my innocence all day long. It was Your pleasure to give me the key on matters my soul could have never understood alone, on marvels beyond me and my knowledge, and for this reason they hound my innocence. There, in every obscure corner they await for an opportunity to plunder my life if that were possible.

23

They call themselves Your people, thinking their mouth is heaven, but what they proffer is false, fallacious and misleading.   I am trying to be bold and show a bold face around but they are constantly gnawing on me. The godless have more charity and humility than those who claim they follow Your Law but never stop judging, and have not the least hesitation to condemn, bringing misery crashing down on me.   Were they godless who judge me, I could put up with that, but THEY, who call themselves Your people! people of God! to whom baptism bounds us together in Your House ....
  I complain, but have I not the right to unload my burden on to You Lord now and then?   Yes, I know I sound and I look like a walking Lamentations Book, but I live my life in innocence, so relieve me for just a while Lord!

Vassula .... do not fret and wail bitterly

24

while being nailed on My Cross, take Me as an example of dignity; soon the darnel will be pulled up from the wheat before any one of you realizes; I have rescued you many times from the snares of your enemies who hoped to destroy you; then, daughter, why do you fear the terrors of the Night?

I am only combatting inside you ....
leave Me alone when I am on My way to the inner room of your soul:

My Dwelling Place;
I have told you before that your soul

25

will leap like on fire every time My Hand falls shattering My rivals that take My place ♡ I am Master and intend to remain your Master; I have set you as My Target for My arrows, no, Vassula, grace does not go without suffering, oh, what will I not do to My closest ones, to My dearest friends! *

Then, allow me to take the words of Saint Theresa of Avila and tell You: no wonder You have so few friends!

all men are weak.... nevertheless, I will reply to

* Jesus was full of delight.

26

your comment and tell you: if your soul only <u>knew</u> what I am offering and doing to you, <u>you</u> would have been the one to ask Me for more trials, sufferings crosses, the lot! – I discipline those I love so do not object to what seems good to Me; you are My jewel and like some precious stone, I cut, carve and form you into the shape I have in Mind; therefore, I tell you, as long as you have breath inside you, you must carry out the work I, Myself, have given you ♡

27

as for those who call themselves Mine yet are offensive when it comes to spiritual matters, I tell them: " if you were blind you would not be guilty, but since you say, ' we see and can tell,' your guilt remains ! how many times will I have to reproach them for their incredulity and obstinacy? come, be in Peace, I am with you for the rest of your journey;

ΙΧΘΥΣ ><>

28.9.92

Ah, My little pupil, I bless you; love

28

Me and glorify Me, for I am three times Holy!

A☧Ω

29.9.92

Lord, our era is guilty of grave blasphemies and, ah, Lord....

say it!

I cannot really see the <u>dawn</u> even of UNITY!

yes?

Maybe what You said Lord, the "soon", it was not my "soon", but Yours! Yours means <u>very</u> LONG, a very long wait!

I shall come suddenly upon you, in a pillar of blazing Fire! a Fire that will

29

change the face of this earth .... come, take courage, My child; every step you take I the Lord bless; if you have the world against you it is because you have seen My Glory; it is because I shared your meal side by side with you; it is because at your house I have entered to glorify My Name again .... have I then no right to be generous? are you reproaching Me because I am generous with your soul? have we not agreed that you will let Me free to do what I please with you? come, you are

30

weak, offer Me your weakness and your wretchedness; ah, one more thing, unless a wheat grain falls on the ground and dies, it remains only a single grain, but My Vassula, if it dies, it yields a rich harvest .... you are My adopted daughter, learn what I mean ♡ let your thoughts, your desires, everything, resemble Mine! so take up your cross and follow Me; I love you to folly so love My Cross too to folly, love Me to folly ♡

A ☧ Ω

31

1. 10. 92

Lord, let Your Holy Face smile again on Your desolate properties*, do not delay, reveal Your Glory now! Many are putting obstacles to obstruct Your messages, come!

My beloved, when your pleading began, a word was uttered and I have come to tell you what it is; do you believe that I am the beloved Son of God, Jesus Christ, speaking to you?

Yes, Lord, I believe!

would I not then see Justice done to you, My chosen one, who supplicate Me day and night? these people are challenging My

* us

32

Power, when the measure of their iniquities is full, they will have to face Me as the

Judge

meanwhile, devote yourself to My Sacred Heart, serve and do not wait to be served so that My Father in Heaven allots you a place in heaven; in being faithful to Me you will undergo great persecutions, but have I not promised you that you will no longer be hungry or thirsty*? so do not be afraid when the tempests rise against you ♡

* Allusion to Ap. 7: 9-17

33

Scriptures have to be accomplished; happy are you who die in Me the Lord! I shall indeed reward you;   ΙΧΘΥΣ 〜◗<

5.10.92

Father, once, before Your Majesty revived the memory of my poor soul, I had forgotten who had made me. The next moment You restored my memory You asked me to lift up my eyes to the heavens, then a ray of Light shone on me and like a consuming fire, Your Spirit rested on me. True Light, Inexhaustible Treasure, You are awe-inspiring, and stupendously Great! How can I not thank and praise You, most Tender Father for resting Your Spirit on my wretched soul and making Your Spirit one with me?

peace be with you; it is I, Yahweh, your Eternal Father, the One who taught you

34

with Wisdom; I am the Holy One who approached you in your misery and healed you; I spoke to you in your sleep and from thereon the scales of your eyes having dropped you have seen the Light; I have taught you, daughter, not to fear Me, but to fear Me only when you reject Me and rebel against Me; I have taught you to dwell in confidence in My Presence showing you My Infinite Tenderness and the Fatherly Love I have for each one of you, I Myself have plucked your sins by the

35

roots and in their place with the space given Me, I planted My graces in you; although your soul leaped like on fire I had to continue My route in your soul and overthrow all the rivals who kept house with you; in My jealous love I replaced those rivals with abundant fruit and henceforth I became your table-companion, your delight! listen now, My daughter, My Own and write and tell My children this: From the depths of My Heart I call to you all! blessed are the ones who have

36

ears to hear; if it were not for My prophets, can you then name Me who foretold the coming of My Son? if you say you live by the Truth and in My Love, how is it then that your generation today cuts out My prophets and persecutes them just as your ancestors used to do? out of My Infinite Mercy a City is being rebuilt for My Own people; will this City renewed be rebuilt on the blood of those you will eternally persecute? today more than ever I am sending you My Holy Spirit to renew you,

37

yet for how long will this generation keep resisting My Holy Spirit? tell Me, can a body live without a heart? learn that My Holy Spirit is the Heart of the Body which is the Church; learn that My Holy Spirit is the Breath of the Church, the Essence of zeal for Me your God; My Holy Spirit is the sweet Manna of Heaven nourishing the poor; happy the man who opens his heart to My Holy Spirit, he will be like a tree along a river, yielding new fruit every season, with leaves that never wither

38

but are medicinal, happy the man who opens his heart to My Holy Spirit, like a crystal clear stream My Spirit shall flow like a river in his heart, renewing him, for wherever this river flows, life springs up, and joy! have you not read: the River of Life, rising from My Throne and from the Lamb will flow down in the middle of the city street? My Holy Spirit will shy away from malicious souls, but will show Himself openly to the innocent, to the poor and to the simple; with

39

great joy My Holy Spirit will envelop these souls and become their Holy Companion and their Guide, and as they walk, their going will be unhindered, as they run, they will not stumble, and should they drink deadly poison they will remain unharmed; should they meet a legion of demons on their route, they will go by unscathed; My Holy Spirit will teach them the sweetness that exhales from Me, the depths of My Eternal Love; My Holy Spirit will take the innocent and make a

40

pact of Love and Peace with them, to become fit and become His partner; My Holy Spirit will lift them and carry them, like a bridegroom carrying his bride across the threshold, He too will carry them behind the walls of the sanctuary where lie fathomless riches and mysteries, mysteries that no eye had seen before; and like a Spouse adorning His Bride with jewels He too will adorn them with imperial knowledge to delight in throne and sceptre; O what will My Holy Spirit not

41

do for you! My Holy Spirit is the zest
of your life, the Royal Crown of Splendour,
the Diadem of Beauty from My Mouth,
the radiant Glory of the Living One,
the Secret Revelation of your creation; My
Holy Spirit is the flavour of your homelies
in My Assemblies and the fulfilment of
your Times .... He is the Flaming Fire of
your heart and the perception of My
Mysteries; My Holy Spirit is the theme of
your praises to Me revealing to your heart
that I Am Who I Am, revealing to

42

your spirit that I am your
                    Abba,
and that you are My offspring, My seed....
blessed be the pure in heart: they shall
see Me; rejoice and be glad and open up
to receive My Holy Spirit so that you too
may delight and hear My Voice! open
your hearts and you shall see My Glory,
and like a child needing comfort My Holy
Spirit will comfort you, whose love for
you surpasses any human love ♡ I, the
Creator of the heavens and ▽ earth

43

tell you, My Holy Spirit is the Spouse of
the Bride, of She who held the Infant
Who was to save you and redeem you, and
in Whom through His Blood you would
gain freedom and forgiveness of your sins;
He is the Spouse of the One Whom He
found like a garden enclosed, holding the
rarest essences of virtues, a sealed fountain, the loveliest of Women, bathed in
purity because of Her unique perfection;
My Spirit came upon Her and covered
Her with His shadow and glorified Me

44

making Her the Mother of God, the
Mother of all humanity and the Queen of
Heaven*; such is the Richness of My Holy
Spirit .... I am showering on all of you
My Holy Spirit, now.... today .... I, Yahweh,
the Almighty am telling you: I am giving
you all this free gift to save you out of
the greatness of the Love I have for you;
Love and Loyalty now descend, I
Yahweh lean down from heaven to embrace

* I want to note that when the Father was dictating
to me this passage concerning Our Blessed Mother,
if He were not God, I would have said He was
exalted, so much was His Joy.

45

all of you, My saving help is offered from above to you; are you willing to comply with My given Law? are you willing to entrust Me with your soul? do not say I am unmoved by your misery and un-responsive to your prayers; if the flames lick up your countries and fires devour your people and if the inhabitants of the earth taste the disgrace of death it is all due to your great apostasy; you have shunned from My Holy Spirit, He who would have clothed you in blessings,

46

He who would have made your heart and flesh leap and sing for joy to Me your God, but you preferred to become homeless, beggared and fatherless and today dwindling away in the shadows of death; how I pity you .... O generation! how much longer can you defy Me? My Love fills the earth, My calls fill the mouths of My envoys and though My grief is acute and My Justice is now brimming over I can still relent and I can accept the homage you would offer Me, I am

47

ready to forgive you through the Blood shed by My Son and through His Sacrifice if you take My Words to heart ♡ soon, very soon now, My Holy Spirit ♡ will blow on you with such force making a mighty sound ring out at the four corners of the earth, as a reminder before all the inhabitants of the earth; then immediately at the sound of My Holy Spirit's Breath, the people of the earth all together would fall on their face to the ground in adora-tion of Me the Lord, the Almighty, the

48

Most High, and in the end the people would bow low before the Throne of the Lamb and receive the Blessing from the Throne ♡ and now, I who created you and I ♡ who formed you, ask you: will I deign to hear your cry of repen-tance?

Α ☧ Ω

49

6.10.92

Lord, when Your words come to me, I devoured them. You have given me this celestial Manna to keep me alive and every Word You utter is my delight. and the saving evidence of Your Love. Your Word is the joy of my soul, the cup of my consolation and the ravishments of my heart.

The world has inherited nothing but Deceptiveness, but Your Word from Your Mouth disinherited the world and all that is within it. Remember how I stood in Your Presence unlawful and naked? and yet instead of decreeing a disaster for my appalling and despicable behaviour, Your utterance pierced these layers of thick dark clouds, and as a king conquering a city, You conquered me placing Your glorious Throne in me. In the parched places of my wilderness You sprang Your Fountain of living Water, showing me Your favour and that from thereon I will be allowed to walk with I AM.

yes daughter, I have never commanded you

50

to sin; realize who is speaking to you and in whose presence you are in! I showed you and to all of you My Heart. I am coming to uproot what the world has sown: deceit after deceit, a harvest of Falsehood! death is creeping below your doors and making its way in silence into your room,* making out of those dearly loved by Me, corpses, winnowing like sheaves left by the reaper, with no one to gather them ♡ My Body is scourged daily from the

* I understood that room, means, soul.

51

sins of the world and, My little bearer, your Lord, who speaks to you now, tells you: I thirst for love ♡ love Me and console this Heart so unloved and so utterly misunderstood! pray for the sinners ....

Lord, our Shepherd, come and gather Your lambs one by one in Your Arms; holding them near Your Sacred Heart. All flesh is weak my Lord, and You Know it, yet, among them there is a list of good men

Vassula, no man is good but God ....

then there is a list of generous souls whose good works should not be forgotten. I know that no one can glorify You as You deserve, but in

52

our weakness and for the sake of Your Love, will You not hurry up Your Return, O Great One, and renew the walls of Your Sanctuary?

you shall be rebuilt!*'

child, so favoured by Me, I have made you a threat to My enemies, these planters have done their planting and they will gather and eat their own fruit....² speak!

Ah, Lord, You have made the heavens and the earth with joy and with great power. You have created us with happiness and loved us with an everlasting love. Let even Your enemies yearn for Your Tenderness. Shine in each heart and turn EVERY heart of stone to You....

*' God, with great majesty uttered these words.
*² I had hesitated, and He stopped.

53

I shall pour out My Spirit on these too, My Vassula; the rebel shall turn into a devout servant, eager to serve Me, eager to worship Me; I shall display My Holiness in every heart and I shall feed them too with My sweet Manna ♡ come, live holy for I am Holy; we, us? Yes, my Lord, we, us....

8. 10. 92

My Vassula, I am your Mother; pethi - mou * remember you are in Our Hearts; live for

* Greek for: my child.

54

Jesus and Me will give you an eloquence of speech to glorify Him; your suffering leads you to sanctification, and I tell you, in all Our grief a ray of consolation penetrates Our Two Hearts and We are filled with overwhelming joy when We see you coming to Us to pray; learn that prayer, love and humility are the strongest weapons against Satan; everyone of you makes part of the renovating process of the Church; but Satan in his fury will toss each one of you against each other if he finds you sleeping;

55

Our Plan is to plant you all together in love and rebuild the Church on Love; you have now seen a dim reflection of how Satan works; I bless you and all those who contribute in this work; pray My Vassula, and although the battle is in its full force, do not fear, I am near you

9. 10. 92

Nassula, listen and write: the devil and his angels are determined to expand their pernicious designs and make of the good things I am sending you venomous alleys;

56

I look to the earth with grief because many ignore the lessons I have been giving you and death is penetrating in many houses, yet, many refuse to understand that evil draws evil ♡ the world, My child, in its apostasy is self - destructing itself ....

Lord?

I Am; yes, confide to Me, unburden your heart and tell Me; I am listening;

Why would that monk want to prevent me from coming to You in this way? I am happy to be in this way with You. You and I, alone; after all it is Your Gift to me....

57

yes, it is My Gift to you and you are My Gift to all; I once said to Martha: "Martha! you worry and fret about so many things and yet few are needed, indeed only one; and it is Mary who has chosen the better part; it is not to be taken from her," and so I am telling him or anyone who comes your way to forbid you from coming to My Feet, like now, to listen to Me, write, and be permanently together: "you worry and fret over many things I do not need! indeed, today I only

58

need one thing:

a "heart to heart conversation,
a prayer without ceasing, in
adoration at My Feet,
unite your heart to Mine; this is the better part ...." and you, My daughter, rejoice! for I have given you freely this Gift; it is not to be taken from you ♡

Famalicão - Portugal -   11.10.92
Message for Padre Joakim Milleihro, the translator and publisher in Portuguese of, 'True Life in God.'

every word he translates caresses My Heart

59

so lacerated, and every step they* take, glorifies Me, I the Lord bless them and their work; I Am is with them A⨯Ω

12.10.92

Portugal - Fatima -

peace be with you; carry My Cross till the end, pray and meditate: enliven My Church;

ΙΧΘΥΣ ⬤—

14.10.92

Portugal - Fatima -

Nassula of My Sacred Heart, in the end every heart will learn the word 'Reconciliation', and

* The nuns helping padre Joakim to publish True Life in God.

60

will accept one another in the heart; unity will be in the heart; ΙΧΘΥΣ ⬤—

(Our Blessed Mother speaks.)   15.10.92
(I had joined the Pilgrims that were going to Poland, Tchekoslovakia, Russia and Rome.)

peace be with you, My Vassula, remember, I am leading this pilgrimage; all I ask from you is to listen to Jesus all that comes your way let it come; allow Jesus to work and speak through you; little one, you have not yet understood how much Jesus loves you; bless Him; My Heart truly is united to His and in the end Our Two Hearts shall

61

triumph; we, us? Yes! Glory be to God!

Russia – Moscow 16. 10. 92

Lord, Almighty, blessed be Your Name; Now, this very day, Your Word is being accomplished. In 1987, You said, 'go to your sister, Russia'; here I am, at her feet. You said, 'love her as I love her'; I am here to love her and if You want me to serve her, I will do it. Just utter Your command.

♡ * .... treasure what I have said to you; realize that My Plan for Russia is great; realize that I will use you for My Glory; My child have My Peace; with you I Am;   ☧

* Here the Lord gave me His order, but it should not be known to the others and to no one yet.

62

Russia – Moscow 18. 10. 92

Shepherd of humanity, overthrow all Kingdoms that do not call on Your Name!
Shepherd, You who lead us with loving care back into the Fold, Your anxious glances do not escape me, the swifter sound of Your Heart-beats have left in my own heart traces of sorrow. No, Lord, my ears are not deaf to Your secret Sighs of grief, leaving my own breath weak. Shepherd, the eyes of my soul are witnessing today something never seen before; no, do not hold Your Head sideways, it is of no use hiding Your distress from me, You have set me too close to Your Heart not to notice Your movements .... and the Branch of the Vine absorbed the sap from the Vine ....

beneath My skin I have placed you*; the heavens will wear away before My creation

* Expression that means that I am in God.

63

wakes .... see how My Passion for mankind reduced Me to?

Can I be of any use to You, my Shepherd? you will pray, you will fast for My Sake, and your footsteps should follow close to Mine; pray that the Father's Hand does not fall at an hour when dreams muster the mind of this generation;

My Lord, my spirit absorbs Your grief, come I beg You, let my heart and those hearts that love You comfort You, and soothe Your pain. The eyes that once saw Your sorrow will never stay dry; were You to pass me, I still should see Your movement and detect Your pain. I am only Your creature,

64

but You have placed me beneath Your skin, without any merits and for no reason. You fostered me. What shall I say then, when You, my God, stand up in front of me, the supreme God, so offended and so grieved? See? I am beneath Your skin, and yet, a mere creature, fashioned out of clay. Have I deserved the warmth of Your Body and Blood, the warmth of Your Heart and Your closeness? No....

do you look forward to your dwelling in heaven, near Me, and making your way in the Light? does your heart long for your permanent home?

Yes! Holy One! Oh yes!

♡ My priest .... you will enter My Court at the accomplishment of your mission;

1

although My Heart longs to take you into the heights of My Sanctuary, I could not take you prematurely, I still have more to say; My beloved, we shall pass the lanes and the street-corners together gathering the dead, you will draw them near Me and I will breathe in them; little by little, therefore, I will wake up the dead so that your Shepherd's sobs cease ....

— O may Your Words find fulfilment!

rise then, spread My Message like a panoply around the world, I am with you, and

2

you shall follow My vigorous stride, work promptly and do not worry, Satan can tear himself to pieces if he wills, but you, for all his rage, will not be silenced or scathed; you will finish your race with Me ♡

A Ω

Russia   Moscow   18.10.92

little one, have My Peace; let nothing take away this Peace I have given you; realize how great is My Plan; I have great events yet to come; this country will honour Me more than any other country;

3

I have already taken one step

in her ....

Vassula, I will ask you to preach to My children of Russia, this will come to you, as I have taught you*; be wise and proceed as I will indicate to you; remain nothing and I shall augment; My Heart is your home ♡ I Am; I ΧΘΥΣ ⟩○

Russia - Moscow -   20.10.92

Russia will honour You in her poverty. Perhaps UNITY will come through her since You say that she will be the one who will glorify You most. Weren't these Your Sighs of Your sacerdotal

* meaning the Lord will bring things to my door-step.

4

Prayer to the Father?

come, write: My Peace I give you;

I am the Resurrection,

and resurrection shall soon take place in My daughter Russia; do not be judge of her sons and daughters so that I will not be compelled to judge you ♡ were anyone perfect among you, you would still count for nothing in My Perfection; soon the Glory will be given to Me in its fulness and Russia will govern the rest of My children in holiness; I, the Lord, am asking you for your prayers,

5

your sacrifices and expiations so that all these things may lead My Russia near Me; in her wretchedness I will show My Mercy, in her weakness, My Power and My Authority, in her nothingness

<u>all that I Am</u>

and in her aridity I shall make Rivers flow out of her, I shall uproot in her all that is not Me and in these empty spaces, plant My Graces in her; I shall plant seeds of Love and Peace ♡

"Russia, it is not long ago since you

6

broke your alliance with Me, burst your bonds and said: 'I will not serve You!' now I shall give you children who will proclaim My Name in Holiness and say: 'blessed is He who restored our sight and touched our heart; blessed is He who changed our ways healing us;' then, with Me in you and you in Me,

<u>you will live</u> ♡

and with Our Two Hearts in your heart you will give Me the Glory foretold;"

Vassula, My bride, for My sake, pray

7

for the full conversion of Russia; I the Lord, bless you My child, never forget that I am He who loves you most; My Heart can be touched .... ΙΧΘΥΣ ><>

Later on that evening I was invited with a friend by a Russian orthodox priest who works for Unity to assist a meeting on Tradition. The Lady president said that anyone who wants to speak from the audience, will have 8 minutes.
The Russian orthodox priest asked the president on a piece of paper which was passed on to her, whether I could speak to the crowd too.
I presume she knew who I was because she sent back a note saying 'no'.
The priest again wrote a second note, sent it to her, and her reply was once more negative.
It was becoming a matter now for the angels to intervene. I called my angel, and asked

8

him to gather the other angels who surround me to go and speak to her angel and make her change her mind.
Just then I felt Jesus intervening, as though He was asking me: "What are you doing!?"
"I am sending my angels..." He said: "I have told you before sending you to Russia that you were going to go only as a pilgrim, this time!"
I suddenly remembered. But I said like a spoilt child: "Oh Lord! please, I will not make a discourse; just give me <u>three</u> minutes, just to introduce Your Message, nothing more. It is such an occasion Lord!" Hardly had I finished my words when the president suddenly sent another note allowing me eight minutes of speech. But the Good Lord nevertheless, gave me ten whole minutes....

21.10.92

Vassula, write*: "... and every tree of the

* The Lord asked me to write from Ez. 17: 24

9

field will learn that I, Yahweh, am the one
who stunts tall trees and makes the low
ones grow, who withers green trees and makes
the withered green; I, Yahweh, have spoken,
and I will do it ♡"
daughter, every time anyone wounds you,
My Heart, an Abyss of Love, opens wide for
you to absorb you in its depths; I repay every
one of your wounds with Tenderness and
Kisses from My Mouth .... daughter, are you
willing to accept the crosses I am giving you?
.... I have asked you a question ....

10

Suffering has become my daily bread, but what
an honour to share it with You. You come
daily into my room to share my meal, side
by side with me. You sup with me sharing
my daily bread.   You are my Sacrificer, pitilessly
You bend Your bow aiming at me and Your
arrows are raining on the Target You have
chosen.   You make my soul leap like on
fire, from Your arrows.   And yet, when I do
not have this bread I ask: ' where is the bread
that burns up one's heart ?'

♡ My generosity and My kindness are not yet
exhausted; the favours I have favoured
you with will be renewed, for My Burning
Love will consume you to ashes, and I
will make your soul drunk to thirst for
My arrows; you shall not be deprived ....

11

so rejoice and exult for to you in turn
My Cup I will pass .... I mean to bring
nation after nation to live under My shadow,
and believe that the Father sent Me,*¹ yes,
the Day will come when all the earthly rulers,
the governors and the commanders, the rich
people and the men of influence, the whole
population,*² will recognize Me as the Christ,
Son of the Living God; and from every
place, men will lift their hands up reverently in prayer and worship, all in one
voice and heart; for this I need victim

*1   Jn: 17: 21
*2   Ap: 6: 15

12

souls, for this I need collaborators, so do not
fear men, My Eyes watch over you; if one
person loves anointing My Name and others
lack charity, challenging Me, to which one
will the Master offer His heritage? My daughter,
be in peace, I resent those who testify My
Word yet scoff and mock Me in others; let them
make their peace with Me; and you, My
daughter, do not wriggle in My Hands,
allow Me to sweep away the particles
hindering My passage in your soul, let Me
proceed without your objecting, you do not

13

need reminders with engraved inscriptions, I want My passage free; I have as you said, favoured you, to hear My Voice; I have allowed your soul to stretch out and touch Me, what have you felt? what did your fingertips feel around My Heart? petals of roses? no? then what did you feel? different bouquets of chosen flowers? oh no, those who receive bouquets of flowers are loved; then what did your hands feel? thorns? yes, and much more than a crown of thorns: you have felt the

14

lance's blade .... I want you to expiate for all those who offend Me and wound Me; I am determined to perfect you by aiming My arrows on you, by bowing you and making you obedient and humble; your soul will learn to endure the ordeal of being openly and publicly calumniated and ridiculed, since you are unable to deign to bow low, My intervention then is necessary; I would not want you to appear to Me in the last minute unacceptable; My very core is yearning for your perfection so do

15

not ever complain about those who calumniate you in written form and in public; your sufferings glorify Me so let your soul thirst for such offences made upon you, what greater gift could I offer a soul who still is so far from perfection? come close to Me and rely on My pardon ♡

ΙΧΘΥΣ 〉⊂—

21. 10. 92

This message was for (...). The Father spoke.

look, presents and gifts I do not receive many, the offering and the generosity of him whom I have chosen to counsel you

16

pleases Me; " beg Me to guide your steps into this task so that you may proceed into the truth, I find My delight when you hear Me; speak of My instructions before My children, tell them that Yahweh, your Eternal Father, Father of all, asks them to seek His Face now and then ....

yahweh continues: А ⳨ Ω

praise Me Vassula, pray and be concerned only for My Interests, I Yahweh bless you from the core of My Heart; I love you!

17

Rome　25.10.92

Altar! I will place on you My Words
hear and write: you are under My Tent,
so abandon yourself each day to Me that
I may do My Will in you; be placid
and willing; you are very precious to Me,
My child; — Vassula, My dove, Wisdom
who has been up to now your Educator will
continue to teach you and tell you what
your duties are: I will appeal from you
love for your sister Russia; I will send
you back to her and with you My Own

18

Heart ♡ Russia is especially dear to Me;
indeed today Russia is like an open field
ready to be sown; her soil is ready to
receive any seed; I have given revelations
through My Spirit to be sown in her;
nobody will be allowed to lay down any
other foundation than My very Own foundation; it is I, God, who designed Russia
for My Glory and it is through her that
light will shine out of her darkness, it
is through her light that your generation's
heart will be enlightened with the know-

19

ledge of My Glory; I shall pour out My
Spirit on the House that I had given
her and I will display My Holiness in her
to honour My Name; it was of her that I
spoke in the past through My little prophets,*
I tell you: all her splendour she once
had I will give in double, for she will put
her whole heart into following Me and seek
My Holy Face once more ♡ no one will
gloat over her for I will lift her to become
the head* of many nations ♡ in her

* Spiritually

　　* Fatima's children

20

poverty, I will rebuild My Kingdom, ah
Vassula! just wait and see!

A ⳩ Ω

1.11.92

Zeal for You devours me, I am Yours Lord;
turn to me please and fill my mouth to
revive me. Rescue me from human tongue....
accept the homage that I offered you now*
I love You Lord to madness.
love Me for those who do not; I Am is
watching over you; little by little I have
raised you, dearest soul, that you may

* I just heard how someone I know is persecuting me.

21

glorify Me; you are to teach this generation
the words: Love and Unity; listen Vassula
of My Sacred Heart, My Love will save
you; puny and despised you will be,
contradicted and disbelieved from within
My House you will be; persecution will be
your daily bread, these will be your com-
pensations on earth, for all these things
will direct your steps into My Kingdom;
your traces left behind will bring many
other souls to Me, therefore, concentrate on
My Own traces and follow Me ♡ I am

22

glad you confided this revelation to My
Mother, I tell you, you could not have
chosen better; My Mother will be your de-
fender, no one will be able to damage
these writings, I have blessed them ♡
so dear to Me, I love you, never doubt
of My Love; I Jesus am with you; I
delight in you ♡ ΙΧΘΥΣ ⩥

5. 11. 92

peace My little one; raised by Me, enter
into My Sacred Heart; you will overcome
your oppressors, yes every single one will

23

fall; I am weak and far from being strong...
keep in your mind that I Am is the
Rock and your strength will come from this
Rock; altar? I will look after you; you
must leave Me free to purify you; blemishes
in your soul sadden Me and are a horror
to Me, My altar I want without blemish,
I want pure; I want to clothe you in
splendid robes; bless Me, I who am your
counsellor; I bless You Lord Jesus.
I need to plunder you and make you poor,
I love poverty; earthborn, have you nothing

24

to tell Me?

I am Your victim and it is with You and into
Your Hands I want to be to be able to feel
what You felt when on earth. I want to
taste You.

I will grant you to taste Me if this is what
you sigh for .... I will, if you allow Me,
subdue you to My Will; .... and you will
learn how great is My Name and how
perfect is the One who made you these
advances .... ΙΧΘΥΣ ⩥

10. 11. 92

peace be with you ♡ today's lands have

25

been totally polluted and have everything but Me; what seems right to the world is abhorrent in My Sight and is already condemned by Me; if the world hates you it is because you love Me, let your testimony be valid in My Eyes and I tell you, your testimony will only be valid were you to sacrifice entirely for the salvation of souls and show your love by laying down your life for your friends and for those you call your enemies, so that when My Day comes you need feel no shame; I, Myself,

26

will provide you with My Strength, in the meantime carry on the work I have given you and shout for joy, rejoice because with My Power I will break through their wall and let everything that had been hidden from you to be exposed to light; your eyes will see crawling before you all sorts of animals and snakes, but do not be afraid of those who kill the body, I tell you they cannot kill the soul, fear him rather who can destroy both body and soul in hell! follow in My Footprints

27

and do not look for honour or praise; if the world takes you for imposters know that you are genuine, for the first one the world took for an imposter was Me; love! and forgive! pray for those who plot incredible schemes against My Holy Spirit and do not judge them lest what is fatal for them, turns to be fatal on you; let Me correct them, let everything you do be planted in love; I shall provide you and fill you with consolations; every thorn in My Body will be removed in the end; love

28

will triumph;

Α ☧ Ω

15. 11. 92

" If only my miseries could be weighed,
   and all my ills be put on the scales!
But they outweigh the sands of the seas;
   what wonder then if my words are wild? "

(Jb 6 : 2,3)

I shiver with horror to think I might be wrong! Will I be found with blame in Your Presence my God? yet I have taken root in You, I saw You standing there, silent, with Your Hand outstretched as someone expecting alms, then I heard a Voice*[1] a Name*[2] was given me and my soul succumbed into My Father's Arms. O God! how I love You!

My child; My child .... how I the Lord love you! I love you to tears .... cease listening to the evil one who tries to destroy

*[1] The Voice of the Father *[2] Yahweh

29

all the good things I have given you;
have faith in My Love, I will never fail
you*¹ .... never*² .... so have My Peace, this Peace
I have given you and know, My child,
that greater love than Mine you will never
meet .... ah My child, cling on the hem
of My robe; I am here and with you ♡

A ☧ Ω

*¹ He said these words almost as a whisper.
*² He whispered this word.

30

19.11.92

Your auxiliary slave is at Your Service.
Vassula of My Sacred Heart, beloved of My Soul,
come to Me; when persecuted enter My Sacred
Heart and taste My Love; among many, I
have chosen you to follow Me into the
Path that leads to Unity; I have made
you My pupil and not only have I
become your Educator and Teacher but I
have become your Spouse; with Me you
will lack nothing beloved;

Do You want me in dictation, Lord?

every minute of your life! every single

31

minute of your life, be with Me! in
prayer, in dictation, in meditation, in
receiving Me in the Holy Eucharist, at the
hours of adoration, prove your love to Me!
prove your thirst for Me, prove your
faithfulness by remaining united in love
with My Heart ♡ be steadfast, dependent on My Strength and always look
forward to meeting Me; ah, little one, have
you not understood? have you not noticed
the greatness of the Love I have for you,
and My friendship? .... and now,

32

while you are still here, join your prayers
with these of the saints and remember,
I know perfectly well what you have in
your heart; I know your needs; everything! you all belong to Me alike
and would I not give My Life all over
again for you were it needed!* ....
here I am sending My Spirit to remind
you of the greatness of My Love, and to
ask you to withdraw from the world
that has everything but Me; for each

* These words were given with much expression
since they came out of His Divine Heart.

33

one of you I have a place in My Sacred Heart; come, unite your heart with My Heart and live Our Messages; I bless each one of you, leaving the Sign of My Love on your forehead; be one!

A✗Ω

27. 11. 92

peace be with you; it is I, Jesus; pray with Me and say:

Father, all I ask from
You now is to strengthen
my faith; Amen

I repeated it with Jesus.

34

Philippines - Manila 29. 11. 92

I am your good Shepherd; I heard your call from above so how could I resist your cry, when I hear laments and your agony? I have come in this way to speak to you and remind your hearts of My request:* have you all reconciled with your brothers with your sisters, with everybody? only a few have .... here I am, sending you word again; I do not come as a Judge, not yet, and if I reproach you, it is

* In 24. 10. 91　the Lord gave a message to the Philippines asking them to reconcile.

35

because of the greatness of the love I have for you .... I am a jealous God and I want prayers, prayers without ceasing; ah, beloved children, if you knew how My Heart is lacerated every time one of you postpones for later on My desires ..... I tell you, I will soon descend in full force with My Holy Spirit to give sight to the blind and take away the sight from those who say they see .... the spirit who is hovering over this world is a rebellious spirit, ruling the world

36

to live a Godless life, thus profaning My Sanctuary; are you not all of you My Sanctuary? delight your Father in Heaven and pray for the Reconciliation of this world; happy the peacemakers when they work for Peace! they will be called children of the Most High; pray that My Church be one; today there is a division in My Church as never before; like Cain and Abel, brothers, yet unlike one from the other; one blood, yet different; one was sincere, the other one not, one was

37

well disposed, the other one was ill-disposed and displeasing Me ♡ one was faithful and devout, the other one treacherous and a rebel : these are today's members in My Church, I have two sorts: one, devout, the other one a rebel. My Church is divided ; I tell you truly that My Kingdom is among you; — My Holy Spirit today is blowing on you all to revive what little is left in you, and to bring the rebels back to their senses; My Holy Spirit of grace is blowing on you

38

My Passionate Love; the sheep that belong to Me will recognize My Voice from far, soon, I shall make disciples shine out, I, your King am blessing each one of you from the core of My Heart; be one !

ΙΧΘΥΣ ⟨°}}}><

29. 11. 92

Our Blessed Mother gives a message to the Filippinos.

like a Mother I come to ask you to listen to your Father ; hear Him and do whatever He asks you to do ♡ I have shown you the Wounds of Our Hearts in a

39

special way; I shall remain with you in this way for only a short time now, but I shall not leave you, you who are the Shepherd's lambs, without making sure that you have shelter and pasture ♡ the world again misjudged the Times and cannot recognize the Signs either; the world does not listen to Our Two Hearts, nor understand Them, they are rejecting Us .... but the hour is near when a Light will shine from above and Our Two Hearts, like Two Lamps

40

shining near each other will revive this world, bringing it from darkness to light; those Two Hearts the world combatted will prevail in the end ! and the kingdoms of the world will pass away and will be replaced by My Son's Kingdom .... this is all very near you now ! when you leave from here *, leave with the Lord's peace and My peace ; ♡

* The Church we were in.

41　　　　　　　　　　　　1. 12. 92

Your word is my delight, my Life and my
hope. What have You found in my
wicked heart to establish Your Throne inside
it? Day and night You show Your favours
to me.

I have established My Throne inside your
heart to save you and to deliver you;
I have established My Throne inside your
heart to reign over you;
I have established My Throne inside your
heart to endow you with My Spirit;
your poverty enchanted Me, your misery
attracted Me; if such favour is shown to
the wicked, will I not much more favour

42

the righteous, oh men of little faith?
I am the First and the Last,' the
Beginning and the end ♡

A ☧ Ω　　　　　　Australia 2. 12. 92

Show me the Light of Your Holy Face, raise
my soul to the heights and let me see You!
compensate Me then and evangelize with
love for Love; every word you will utter
for the glory of My Holy Name, will be
blessed so that like a dove it will flutter
and reach where it will make its home;
ic*, Jesus ♡　*"ic" are initials found on Greek
icons where Jesus is portrayed. IC,
is short for 'Jesus' ICOUΣ.

43

compensate Me and give Me your time,
your mind, your hand and your heart
to use for My Glory; then watch My Lips,
touch My Heart and write; never let go
of the hem of My clothes! ♡ aℛw

Just when Jesus signed and sealed this
message, He said to me in a whisper:
'Sarajevo* shall perish.'

Before my mission in Australia — 3. 12. 92

look at Me! receive the One who loves
you most! My lamb, I am with you

* Sarajevo is a town in ex Yougoslavia. Three
days after the Lord said this, on the 5.Th 12. 92,
Sarajevo was attacked.

44

and My Word will be brought into your
mouth and It shall cut and pierce
their hearts; good and bad will hear
you; you will preach and teach the Knowledge I Myself have given you through
these years; perseverance? is that
what you need, child?

Yes, my Lord!

I will keep you company to revive your
soul; My presence will encourage your
heart and you will persevere; we
are partners, are we not?

45

We are!

then do not be afraid; I and you, you and I and the power of My Holy Spirit will lift you and will whisper and remind you the sound Teachings I have given you; do not fear, I have never failed you; I will give you an eloquence of speech to give honour to your King ♡ ΙΧΘΥΣ

Australia   3. 12. 92

Christ, You are the theme of my praise in our assemblies. I have treasured the instructions You have given me from Your Lips. I invoke You now Sacred Heart to help me

46

display the Fathomless Tenderness, the Love of the Almighty God, Our Father, the delicacy of Your Own Sacred Heart and the Infinite Riches of Your Spirit.

I tore the Heavens and came down into your room; so now join in the saints' choir and sing with your whole heart, yes, wholeheartedly; My glory will be shared with the innocent souls, the poor and those who united their hearts to Mine; I will display My Love and show everyone that greater love than Mine you will not meet; see what you have? Love

47

Himself comes to your room to speak to you; you have seen Me face to face; I, Jesus bless you from the core of My Heart; - feel loved- I, Jesus Christ am resurrected and alive and am near you, now IC

Australia   7. 12. 92

Just before the meeting, God, our Father gave me this message.

write: tell them that I am the Most Tender Father; tell them how I lean to reach them, now;

Love and Loyalty now descend to

48

embrace all of you, to renew you, to revive you and lift you up from the lethargy that covers this earth; do not say I am too far to reach, unmoved by your misery and unresponsive to your calls; if the flames lick up your countries and fires devour the people of the earth it is all due to the great apostasy that seized nation after nation infiltrating in the heart of My Law; this apostasy beggared you and made you believe you are fatherless ... how I pity you! O

49

generation, for how long must I wait? My warnings and My calls echo the earth and though My grief is acute and My justice now brimming over I can still relent and I can accept the homage you would offer Me; I am ready to forgive you through the Blood shed by My Son and through His Sacrifice, if you take My Words to heart; I who created you out of Love ask you:

will I hear from you your cry of repentance? ... daughter, glorify Me and

50

reveal My Holy Face with love to everyone! I bless you and everyone accompanying you;

A ☧ Ω

9. 12. 92

peace be with you, favoured by My Father, be My Echo! establish My Kingdom in Australia, sow My seeds of Love every-where and in all directions; do not delay and answer to all requests given you; I will give you enough strength to promul-gate My Message .... demonstrate the convincing power of My Spirit, demonstrate

51

how My Spirit uplifts, instructs and reveals the depths of the Truth and of the Eternal God; demonstrate to the unlearned the reality of spiritual things given by the Spirit and uncover the Knowledge given by My Spirit; demonstrate the full power of My Spirit, how He develops, testifies and gratifies the poor, the simple, the humble but shies away from the rich, the wise, the proud who assess My Spirit with their natural understanding and evaluate everything in terms of their spirit ♡

52

Vassula, evaluate your spiritual growth and do not doubt of My grace; I, Jesus am your Teacher and Master; never doubt; ic; have My Peace IXΘΥΣ ⋈

Adelaide - Australia 10. 12. 90
(Before the meeting)

feel happy that I have saved you; allow Me now to use you for My glory; bring My children to understand the Knowledge I have passed on to you; carry on the way you proceeded in the other assemblies; smile at Me, My Love for you is

53

greater than you think! come, by grace
I lifted you and millions of others, allow
Me now to guide your step, ic ♡

Jesus!
I Am;

Do not go yet!
why? do you wish Me to remain?*
ah, you see? I will never impose Myself
on you ....

* I could not answer Him. Jesus as a rule asked
me to be with Him for half an hour before any
meeting. Today I had come late. Time was
pressing and I wanted to get ready too.

54

Jesus?
I Am;
Speak to me please.
Love loves you; love Me and thirst for Me
as I thirst for you; caress Me now and
then by allowing Me to speak in your
heart; understand, soul, that you are
not meant for this world but My Own
Kingdom in Heaven, so renounce all that
holds you to the world and look for
heavenly things; come; we, us?
Yes Lord!   ΙΧΘΥΣ ><>

55

13.12.92

Our Father, who art in Heaven hallowed be
thy Name .... Our Father, whose love is
revealed to the least of us, have mercy on
Your creation! You have given us as a
free gift: our liberty, to use as we please,
but we have turned our liberty against us.
Like a razor-blade in an infant's hand, we
use it, hacking ourselves to death ... O come!
and turn our attention to Your Holy Name,
or we will slice ourselves to pieces!
I invoke You God Almighty in our troubles,
will You rescue us, or will You hide from
my petition?

daughter, you are in charge of My Message,
and I have been sending you in the world
from nation to nation to cry out repentance
and reduce this wilderness; indeed, the crowds
throng around you; it has come to their

56

ear that I Am is speaking, and nation
after nation is talking about you. they say
to each other: "let us go and hear
what God is saying;" they come in thousands and sit down in front of you
and listen to your words, but who acts
on them? as far as they are concerned,
you are like a love song beautifully sung
to music; your words enchant them, but
who among them puts My Messages into
practice? have they understood the words:
reconciliation, peace, love and unity?

57

when brimstone and devouring flames will take place - and they are very near you now - they will learn that I had sent a prophet among them; from the beginning I had given you My Commandments; I had asked you to love Me, your Lord, with all your heart, with all your soul, and with all your mind; today I am asking you to allow Me to touch your soul so that your heart will be able to praise Me and tell Me that neither death nor life, no angel, no prince, nothing that exists, nothing still to come,

58

not any power, or height or depth, nor any created thing, will ever come between you and your love to Me; I am your Strong- hold; know that My Love is revealed even to the very least of you; do not search your salvation in the light of the world, since you know that the world cannot give you life; soon My Throne and of the Lamb will be in its place and your soul will be renewed with My Transcendent Light, because I, your Father, intend to restore the memory of your soul and make your

59

heart sing to Me the word Abba - Father! I tell you, you do not belong to the world, so why do you still allow yourselves to be deceived over and over again? _ since the foundations of the earth I have called you by your name but when I proposed Peace, universal Peace, nearly all of you were for war; yet, I am pouring out My Holy Spirit now to remind you of your true foundations and that all of you are My seed; but today My seed is filled up with dead words .... I am the Holy

60

One who held you first; for how long will your soul resist Those Eyes who saw you first? and for how long will your soul deny My distressed calls? many of you are still fondling the Abomination of the Desolation in the most profound domain of your soul; can you not see how the Viper repeatedly is deceiving you in the same way he deceived Adam and Eve? Satan is suggesting to you, untiringly and subtly to cut off all your heavenly bonds that bond you to Me, your Father in

61

heaven; he mesmerized the memory of your soul to make you believe you are fatherless thus creating a gulf between you and Me, your God; Satan wants to separate you from Me and cut off your umbilical cord that unites you to Me in which Rivers of Life flow into you ♡ generation, you have still not set your minds for Me; when will you decide to return to Me? do you want to pass this era's threshold by blazing fire, by brimstone and devouring flame? how could your soul trade My

62

My Glory for a worthless imitation that the evil one offers you daily; ask Me for your daily bread and I shall give it to you! why are you all so willing to listen to the Viper? you and I know that Satan is the father of lies, then why are you still listening to him? I, your Creator, am your Father and I am calling you back to Me; believe in My distressed calls; will your soul continue to befriend the Rebel, or will you deign to come down from your throne and repent? it is for

63

you to decide; — there is not much time left — I am reminding you to beware of the false teachers and the false prophets who induce in your soul desolation and misinterpret the gospels, telling you that the Holy Spirit is not with you to remind you of your foundations nor of where you come from; they have already made a desolation out of your soul and dug a vast gulf between you and Me your Father; do not let them expand this desolation in your soul and mislead you into

64

believing I have left you orphans; these false prophets have made out of My Son, Jesus, a liar and out of the gospels an echoing cymbal, empty with emptiness; they made out of My Word a gaping grave; so beware of those false teachers, who tell you that My Holy Spirit cannot descend to perform in you miracles and wonders; beware of them who condemn My Holy Spirit who in your days more than anytime, reminds you of your foundations; beware of them who keep

1

up the outward appearance of religion but reject the inner power of it, the inner power that is My Holy Spirit; and if any-one of you is calumniated and dejected because you are witnessing the Truth, turn to your Holy Mother; She will console your soul and provide you with courage; if the world inflicts on you impressive wounds, turn to your Mother and she will dress your wounds with her Maternal Love and Affection; like She took care of My Beloved Son, your Holy Mother will take care of you too; in your

2

misery and distress She comes flying to you and takes you into Her Heart, that same Heart who conceived your Saviour; your Holy Mother in Heaven will teach you to enlarge My Kingdom on earth by teaching you to love Me; so let love be the principle of your life; let love be your root; allow Me, your Father, to bond you to Me; allow Me to touch your soul. come to Me and thrust yourself into My Arms. what greater bliss than being held by those Hands that created you? place your ear on My Mouth, this Mouth that

3

breathed in you through your nostrils: Life, and from the dust of the soil I revived you to conquer the earth; I touched you and asked you to listen to My Word since then; come, you must set your heart right, renounce the iniquities that stain your soul and with all your heart

HALLOW MY NAME

4

17.12.92

Lord, Father and Educator of my life, who disciplined my heart, You who ravished my soul with a single one of Your glances, do not hide Your Holy Face from me, return, that I may contemplate on You; O Jesus, come! come to us where light itself is like the dead of night!

your King is here .... pray with Me to the Father:

Father,
I consecrate myself
in soul and body to Your service,
so that Your Eyes and Your Heart
never leave me;
set Your Royal Throne inside me

5

and give me Your orders,

make me advance in purity of heart,

to accomplish

all that You have given me;

amen ♡

daughter, I will complete ♡ this journey with you; do not be afraid; for your part, if you walk with Me at My pace, you shall not lack; if you turn away from Me, I will double your crosses to save you .... *

* I understood that if I will not follow Him, He will also leave me and with crosses only. Seeing that I misunderstood Him, He added the following sentence.

6

whoever returns to Me, I shall not turn him away; listen to My Heart-beats so that their sound spare you any thought of rebellion; I, Jesus, bless you; ΙΧΘΥΣ ⟩○⟨

Read in unity week in Los Angeles + Sacramento, 21.12.92

daughter of My Sacred Heart, I would like you to write; hear from heaven My Voice ♡ My Words of Reconciliation, Peace and Unity have not been heard nor have they been respected, I have spoken once and I will not speak again; I will add nothing new;

7

Lord, it is not easy apparently *

I want your voice to thunder this time in January! *2 I want your voice to thunder as loud as ever! you will speak on My behalf; let the whole world hear: the days are now counted, there is not much time left and grace that enfolded mankind shall come abruptly and all of a sudden at its end .... this will be done so that the world realizes how great was My Mercy and My

* I wanted to say : ' to unify the dates of Easter'. This is what those working for unity had told me. But Jesus cut me and continued, with power in His Voice.
*2 Month of Unity.

8

Goodness that had flowed down from above year after year; .... tell those who work for unity to look up at the skies; see how far they are from the earth? this is how far their hearts are from one another; this is how far they are apart, ♡ * when will they all pass a decree by unanimous vote to celebrate the feast of Easter all in one date?

I am weary of hearing their noble language, perhaps it is suitable and eloquent for

* Jesus here seems to direct their step suggesting what they would have to do.

9

them but to Me it sounds like a stroke on a gong, because it is empty with emptiness; I have come to talk to them, first, out of concern, then out of pity, but no one yet to this day has lowered his voice to hear My Voice; alas for you, who say you are at My service yet prevent My Kingdom from finding unity and stability! but it is not you who will bring My Kingdom together.... for you do not understand anything and never will .... if you, in spite of My heavenly calls, did not sound the depths

10

of My Heart, how would you unravel the arguments of My Mind, how can you fathom the Riches of My Sacred Heart? I have not spoken in parables, nor have I spoken in riddles, I have taken plain words to speak to you; I reprimanded the officials and I collected them together to talk to them*¹ but have they observed the prompting of My Heart? their duty was to make an official appeal; I reprimanded the authorities*², I had not come that day*³ to attack them, but to

1+3* using me as His mouth piece.
2* at the World Council of Churches.

11

offer them oil to fill up their lamps, lest further harm be done to My Church; how many of them stretched out their hands to heaven, calling Me? do they realize how, twice*¹ My Blood is shed like water?
 — may My groans reach their ears this time.....
what My right Hand planted has been severed, in two, then in three, then hacked; where is the entire vine*² I had planted? ....
 there was once a vine, every season I expected it to yield grapes; it covered

1* the two Easters: Roman Catholic and Orthodox.
2* could be interpreted as Church, or God's people.

12

valleys, mountains and extended beyond the seas, because it had taken root in My own property, in My own inheritance; I had spread its branches to reach to the four corners of the earth and fill the world with fruit; but instead of keeping it, they neglected it, allowing thorns and briars to multiply around it, choking branch after branch, shoot after shoot; that chosen plant My right Hand had planted has been levelled now to the ground and the beauty and glory, and the fruit it gave have now fallen down like

13

rotten fruit; there is no need then to swell
with pride, and cease to have proud eyes in
case your errors multiply and your deeds
recoil on your own head; I have come to
fill your lamp with oil, light your lamp
and use it now so that you see where you
are going; whosoever neglects to light his
lamp this time and use it, it will be taken
away from him and given to someone else;
let them pray and say these words:

O Lord, You who stand among us,
shepherd us;

14

set Your Royal Throne in
the middle of Your vine
and give us Your orders;
O Holy Lord of all holiness

purify us
so that we preserve the integrity
of Your House and Your vine,
lovingly intervene and protect
what Your right Hand cultivated;
we have failed You,
but we know,
we believe

15

and we trust,
that You will open wide Your
Gateway,
to let the River of Life flow
on Your vine,
and once more from it will
sprout branches that will
bear fruit and become a royal vine,
more kingly than ever before because
Your Holy Spirit
the giver of Life
will overshadow it ♡   amen

16

and you, My Vassula, your sufferings will
teach you to be patient; have you not heard
that patience brings perseverance and perseverance brings hope? and this hope, upon
this hope will raise My Kingdom; let every
part of yourself now glorify Me; My Holy
Spirit marked you with My Seal, so do
not be afraid; pastors, priests, teachers,
bishops and cardinals will recognize the
Shepherd's Call and I will renew their
mind so that their old self is crushed
and they will fully realize that I am

17

on My Way back to transfigure the whole
of My creation in the goodness and holiness
of the

Truth;

A ☧ Ω

come, My daughter, My precious one, I Am is
with you ♡

6. 1. 93

Jesus? Beloved One of the Father, my country's*¹
fields are ravaged*² they have now become
the haunt of the lizard and the spider,
are You no longer there? Are You no longer
in this nation? Why does it make no
progress? Why are You leaving them far
behind? Death has creeped in under their doors...
*¹ Greece   *² spiritually

18

Son of the Almighty God, when will You display
Your Holiness in this nation? ... "Vassilia
mou, yiati kles?"*¹

I weep on her excessive pride ... how am I
to deal with their excessive pride? they do not
listen to My Spirit and are following the
dictates of their own proud hearts;

Truthfully, Lord of all Holiness, am I not doing
my best to serve You, am I not interceding
for Unity? Can I bend iron with my bare
hands?*² Your Fire though can do it.
Your Wealth and Your Treasures of Your
Sacred Heart can do it.

*¹ Greek: "My King, why do You weep?"
*² The iron rods of my vision repainting the 3 Christ-
ian Churches.

19

then I will have to ask more from you ....
I will have to ask more from you; all
that you give Me will be to bind you all
together in love, and enlighten your hearts
so that your spirit may open to My Spirit
who will teach you the depths of your
Father in Heaven, and the hidden jewels
of Wisdom ♡

Poverty is at Your Feet, to serve You
Almighty One.

yes! trust Me; I will always uphold
you, so do not fear; .... look at Me ....

20

My palate is drier than parchment and
the Father will not bear this sight much
longer; the world is offending Him and
His whole Kingdom ♡ the world has
become so wicked, and My Arm cannot
much longer hold away His Arm from
falling upon you; * .... iron can be melted,
so do not lose courage ... do not
forget that I have posted you with a
sword in your hand, to flash like

* Suddenly our Lord stopped, and looked at me,
as if He remembered something, then spoke.

21

lightning; for the proud, these News, I have given you to carry, displease mightily their heart; They trouble their spirit and cause their knees to tremble; as for your nation, I will melt it down as one melts iron: with Fire ♡ ... and they will advance into holiness;

(Message to someone from the Sacred Heart)
Something* which has existed, can never die, Something which revives fervour and brings visible life in My Church will

* The Sacred Heart.

22

never extinct; you are witnessing the revival of My Sacred Heart with your own eyes and of the One whom you say: "I know Him and I love Him;" what is being carried out today does not go without suffering and sacrifice; I will keep alive the Devotion of My Sacred Heart and all that I have taught surrounding it; this is My Own promise; you have been given to witness the revival of My Sacred Heart so that you could give your testimony; to be

23

the sacrifice of the One who takes your sins away is a privilege; I accept the testimony you are giving Me in My Spirit; so what you are seeing with your own eyes is the fulfilment of your times ♡

Eve of Unity week - Los Angeles 17. 1. 93

Lord, I pray as You have prayed: may we all be one, as the Father is in You and You in Him, so that the rest of the world may believe it was the Father who sent You; for this I pray too for the sheep who are not of Your Fold, that they too will listen to Your Voice, I pray for the Moslems, the Jews and others that they may come to love You from today onwards.
Amen

24

I have heard you, I have heard you, My friend ♡ in the end everyone will worship Me; ΙΧΘΥΣ ⋊—

Sacramento 18. 1. 93
Today is my birthday and the first day of Unity week. It was also once the Feast of Peter's Chair. Today I have been invited to speak at the Cathedral of the Blessed Sacrament by the very holy bishop Francis A. Quinn. In the afternoon just before my meeting, the people who invited me offered me a present. When I saw it I felt that it came from Jesus. For He had said to me these words on the 21st October 1992: ... " rejoice and exult for to you in turn My Cup I will pass ... I mean to bring nation after nation to live under My shadow, and believe that the Father sent Me; Yes, the Day will come when all the earthly rulers, the governors

25

and the men of influence, the whole population, will recognize Me as the Christ, Son of the Living God; and from every place, men will lift their hands up reverently in prayer and worship, all in one voice and heart ..." and this is what they offered me: a gold plated Chalice. Engraved on it are these words:

That they all may be one
Feast of Christian Unity
January 18 1993

Then the two bishops that were present celebrated mass after my talk. The choir sang in the cathedral and everything was majestic. They used my Chalice during that mass for Unity, consecrating the Precious Blood of Jesus inside it.

When I was giving my talk in the Cathedral, and was looking at the crowds that had amassed, an estimated 1800 people,

26

I felt sad. There I was, sent by the Lord, to give a speech on Unity and facing perhaps 98% Roman Catholics; but of the men of my people* not one was with me; there were even Moslems and Jews in the Cathedral .... But the Lord kept His surprise gift for my birthday till later on. — Just before mass, in walks an Orthodox priest with his assistant. After mass he asked to talk to me. We met at the sacristy and I understood what the Lord was saying to me: " Russia will be the country who will glorify me most." He was a Russian Orthodox priest...

In the darkness of our division a tiny light of hope will shine of unity. This little light of hope is Russia. Unity will come through Russia and

* Greek Orthodox. (I heard that the Greek bishop had forbidden the Greek Orthodox to come to my meeting.)

27

she will glorify God! I told the Russian priest that he was my birthday present from Jesus. His name is fr. Vassili which is the male name of my name, Vassula.

The other sign that Unity will be brought by Russia was that when I asked the Lord to choose an opening prayer, He chose the prayer of a Russian priest: fr. Sergius Bulgakov. He had asked me to open at random and I did, and my eyes saw first this prayer, that I wrote on December 29, 1989. Here it is again:

O Jesus Christ, our Lord and
          Saviour, thou didst promise
to abide with us always.
Thou dost call all Christians to
draw near and partake of Thy
Body and Blood. But our sin
has divided us and we have
no power to partake of

28

Thy Holy Eucharist together.
We confess this our sin and we pray Thee,
          forgive us and help us
to serve the ways of reconciliation,
according to Thy Will.
          Kindle our hearts with the fire
of the Holy Spirit. Give us the
spirit of Wisdom and faith, of
daring and of patience, of humility
and of firmness, of love and of
repentance, through the prayers of
the most blessed Mother of God
and of all the saints.   Amen.

2.2.93

(I called the Lord but I could not hear Him. It made me sad. Suddenly the silence was broken by the sound of His step* And He spoke to me reproaching me.)

* (Figurative)

29

My Spirit is upon you; day and night I have been waiting for you! *' respect My rules! why do you hold back our en- counters? now you say, " how long will this last*²?" when only a few minutes went by; whereas I, I have been waiting for you several days! until when will I put up with you? you say, your joy lies in being close to Me; wretched you are for good! puny

*' For three days I did not go to them in this way.
*² His absence and His silence.

30

little creature, do not forget who holds you on your feet; I have treated you kindly and I have been your Support; explain then to Me your absence!

Give the poor and needy another chance! I delight in nothing else on earth than Your Presence!

choose then to be with Me! I called you to My Heart, I have not called you to administration;

But who will do the work?

you have not admitted your sin! *

* The Lord was more severe here than before.

31

yes, I sinned for not keeping Your rules; and for not being faithful to Me, say it! and for not being faithful to You.

say:
I will praise my Lord and
my soul will live for Him alone
and I will serve Him alone, and
my lips will sing for Him alone,
and my heart will
pay attention to Him alone, and
now, my heart will beat for
Him alone;
amen; *

* I repeated it after Him.

32

can the dust praise Me? can it proclaim praises to Me? no, not unless My Spirit lives inside this dust; without Me you are nothing; the light in your eyes comes from My Light; I will teach you to obey Me for I will level you to the ground; how else will I be seen? I mean to progress you into holiness ♡ I will crown all My plans with success, so do not deny Me from meeting you; do your work as far as you can, but take care not to neglect the better part; rely on Me to give you

33

support and reinforce you; pray; we, us?

ΙΧΘΥΣ ⟍⟍⟋

3. 2. 93

Lord my God, You are known to be quick in generosity for the poor and for the needy. You are known to fill the mouths of the hungry and for those who stretch out their hands to You. — You lift the needy giving them a royal place with the elect into Your celestial court. You place the weak into Your House. You are known to overthrow kings and kingdoms when they become an obstacle to Your Word. Lord of Tenderness, You look on wretchedness with compassion sending them Wisdom to be their Educator and teach them to walk in Your Presence and enjoy Your favour. Many hound me and oppress me but Your Wisdom taught me that

34

everything is for Your greatest Glory! Unjustifiably men hound me, waiting for me and for the appropriate hour to strike me, Your child, but You are such Joy to me that no matter what men may do to me, I will persevere to proclaim Your Name with Joy. You are such Joy to me that no man, yes, no man can take my eyes away from You. You are immersing perpetually my soul with joy! For You have plunged my soul in a baptism of Love, in a baptism of Consuming Fire leaving my heart ablaze. You have lavished my soul with a vast treasure: that of Your Sacred Heart.

My child, your endurance will earn you your life; your love and patience will win

35

your place in heaven; My child, My child, 'let your portion be Me'; glorify Me and proclaim to the nations the greatness of My love ♡ fear no one, I am before you; raise your eyes and look at Me .... *

I am going to save My people and I will take men from every nation, every race and every language by their sleeve and ask them: " do you want to follow Me? " and they will say: " we want to go with

* I raised my eyes and this is what I saw: Christ's Holy Face smiling.

36

You, since we have now learnt the Truth," and I will bring one after the other back to live in My Heart! I mean to bring peace in each heart; yes! the vine I had planted in the past will give its fruit for My Glory; I will not be slow nor will I ignore the cries of the faithful ♡ if one man builds My Church while another one pulls it down on whom will the fury of My Father pour out in the Day of Judgement? hear Me: I have formed you and educated you

37

to revive My Church and bring unity among brothers; I created you, Nassiliki* and have called you by your birth-name to be Mine and to come freely into My Presence any time and anywhere you may be;*² I want you close to Me; O child so favoured by My Father! if I have chosen you to reveal to you the Father and mark you with Our Love and if My Holy Spirit breathed in you reviving you, filling your soul with His Light, transfiguring the

¹* My official birth name.
²* in this special way.

38

Darkness in you into Light; Nassiliki, it is so that the nations see through you My Mercy and My Love; you may ask yourself, "why me? why has all this happened to me?" I tell you, because of your great misery and your astounding weakness; My Heart, an Abyss of Love pitied you; it could have been anyone; do not stand bemused in front of Me! do you not know your Saviour anymore? who is there to pity My people if it is not Me? when hordes of nations fall

39

continuously into apostasy and the crown of terror is on every head and when de-bauchery is ruling their heart, how can I remain silent? godlessness has spread throughout the world, am I to remain silent? tell them, "happy is the heart who will make peace with his brother*, for he will be called, child of the Most High; happy is the heart who will stop wandering in the night and will reconcile truly with his brother*, not only will

* here it means humanity.

40

he enjoy My favour but truly, I will reveal to him the Inexhaustible Riches of My Sacred Heart! so that people around him, astounded by his radiant beauty will say, "truly, God is hidden with him;" and you, daughter, never part from Me; I, the Lord, will shep-herd you till the end ♡ come;

18. 2. 93

Lord, how long will you allow them* to defy You? When I will speak the next time to them,

* The Greek Orthodox ecclesiastics.

41

I will raise a gale!

They scorned Your advice in the ecumenical centre (in Mexico city)*; got up and left in the middle of the meeting. And as You Know, the greatest oppositions in the World Council of Churches and who did not want my presence there, nor a meeting, were from my own.

but I the Victor will bend them double.... look Vassula-of-My-Passion, have My Peace, search no one else but Me! soul-of-My-Passion, go out to the nations and leave the oppositions to Me, I shall make those that oppose Me get up from their Seats

* All were there. The Greek Orthodox came Late, listened for 20 minutes while I read Jesus' messages of unity, then got up enraged and left.

42

and bend them double; trust Me; go out to the nations and remind everyone of My Love and that Jesus means Saviour, Redeemer and that the greatness of My Love for you all, surpasses everything ... do not look to your left nor to your right, remember how My Father seized by your misery gave you His Peace so that you forward this Peace to everyone; My Father, moved by your astounding weakness revealed His Face to you and through you to others; My Holy Spirit enraptured by your

43

nothingness triumphed over you, installing His Throne in you to rule over your soul, and I filled your heart with the Riches of My Sacred Heart; soon, beloved of My Soul, a white linen will cover you and I Myself shall wrap you in My Heart, engulfing you in My Light ♡ so My child-of-My-Burning-Passion allow Me to use your little hand for just a while longer, ♡ write: I have stepped out of Heaven ♡ to reach you, but have you listened to Me? I have stepped out

44

of My Throne to come all the way into your room to court you and remind you that you are heirs to My Kingdom; I have stepped out of My Dwelling Place and have taken the wilderness in search of you; the Master of the heavens has not denied you His Love, never! I have allowed your eyes, creation, to look on a King in His Beauty, to attract you, to honour My Name I have roused the dead to preach to you My Kingdom; where is your response? and you who talk about Unity, do you think

45

empty words will unite you? who of you is ready to shed all his comforts and follow Me? tell Me, who of you will be first to end My Agony and My groans for Unity and Peace before the Hour comes? this Hour that leaves all My angels trembling; who among you is the soul who will grain the nations with seeds of Love and Peace? who for My Sake will faithfully follow the Light invoking My Name day and night? who of you all will be the first to place his feet into My blood-

46

stained Footprints? are you sincerely seeking Me? see, the days are coming when I am going to come by thunder and Fire, but I will find, to My distress, many of you unaware and in deep sleep! I am sending you, creation, messenger after messenger to break through your deafness, but I am weary now of your resistance and your apathy; I am ever so weary of your coldness; I am weary of your arrogance and your inflexibility when it comes to assemble for unity; you filled

47

and overflowed now the Cup of Stupor; intoxicated by your own voice you have opposed My Voice, but it shall not be forever, soon you shall fall for you have opposed My Voice by your voice's misleading nonsense, naturally My Church is in ruin because of your division; you are not applying My advice nor are you practising My desires for lack of faith, but I will expose your heart to you and to the whole world, I shall expose how secretly you were planning to destroy My Law; * the

* Very gravely, Jesus said what follows.

48

sixth seal is about to be broken *[1] and you will all be plunged into darkness and there will be no illumination for the smoke poured up out of the Abyss will be like the smoke from a huge furnace so that the sun and the sky will be darkened by it; *[2] and out of My Cup of Justice I will make you resemble snakes, vipers, I will make you crawl on your belly and eat dust *[3] in these days of darkness; I will crush you to the ground to remind

*[1] Ap. 6:12   *[2] Ap. 9:2   *[3] Gn. 3:14

49

you that you are not better than vipers ....
you will suffocate and stifle in your sins;
in My anger I will tread you down, trample
you in My wrath! see? My four angels
are standing anxiously now around My
Throne, waiting for My orders; when
you will hear peals of thunder and see
flashes of lightning know that the Hour
of My Justice has come; the earth will shake
and like a shooting star, will reel from its place,
extirpating mountains and islands out of their

* Is: 13:13

50

places, entire nations will be annihilated,
the sky will disappear like a scroll rolling
up*¹, as you saw it in your vision,
daughter*²; a great agony will befall on
all the citizens, and woe to the unbeliever!
hear Me: and should men say to you
today: " ah, but the Living One will
have Mercy upon us, your prophecy is
not from God but from your own
spirit"; tell them: although you are
reputed to be alive, you are dead; your

*¹ Ap. 6:14   *² 21, 7, 90 Notebook 44

51

incredulity condemns you, because you refused
to believe in My time of Mercy and prohi-
bited My Voice to spread through My
mouthpieces to warn and save My
creatures, you shall die too as the bad;
when the Hour of Darkness comes, I will
show you your insides; I will turn your
soul inside out and when you will see
your soul as black as coal, not only
will you experience a distress like never
before, but you will beat your breast
with agony saying that your own darkness

52

is far worse than the darkness surrounding
you; as for you, *(...) that is how I
shall display My Justice to the nations
and all nations will feel My sentence when
this Hour comes; I will make human life
scarcer than ever before; then when My
wrath will be appeased, I will set My
Throne in each one of you, and together
with one voice and one heart and one
language you will praise Me, the Lamb ♡
this is enough for today My Vassula;
do not be bitter with your own people,

* concerns me alone.

53

and do not, soul, trouble your heart either;
I shall show you to the world as a sign
of unity; you are contradicted and rejected
but you know now why: because unity
is unwelcomed, as Love is unwelcomed in
many hearts ♡ sincerity is missing ....
come, we, us?   Yes my Lord...

ΙΧΘΥΣ ⵜ

19.2.93

peace My beloved; are you one with Me?

Make my spirit one with Your Spirit.
Only You can do it Lord.

54

I am glad that you are conscious of
your "nothingness" and that without
Me you can do nothing ♡ lean on
Me and I will attract ♡ your soul
to Me; Love is near you and My
Spirit upon you ♡   allow Me to
continue yesterday's Message; hear Me:
tell them that mercy and wrath
alike belong to Me, who am Mighty
to forgive and to pour out wrath;
My mercy is great, but My severity
is as great; (God asked me to

55

write this passage from Ecclesiasticus 16: 11, 12.)
you see daughter, I will soon reveal
My Justice too ♡ My Plan has a
determined time; My Merciful calls
have also a determined time; once this
time of Mercy is over, I will show
everyone, good and evil that My severity is as great as My Mercy, that
My wrath is as powerful as My
forgiveness ♡ all things predicted
by Me will pass swiftly now;
nothing can be subtracted from

56

them; I have spoken to you of the
Apostasy, Apostasy that "bound" *
the hands of My best friends,
disarming them because of its velocity
and its measure; have I not said
that cardinals will oppose cardinals
and how bishops will go against
bishops and that many are on the
road to perdition?   they have, in
their endless battle, weakened My
Church; today this spirit of rebellion

* It means they were helpless.

57

thrives inside My Holy Place; do you
recall the vision I had given you of
the vipers crawling all over the
Holy Sacraments on the altar? have
I not revealed to you how many of
them oppose My pope*¹? and how
they push him aside*²? I have already
given you a detailed account of the
Rebellion inside My Church;*³ My
faithful friend, allow Me to stop here;
we shall continue later on; stay

* ¹ Pope John Paul II   *² Previous message.
*³   12.9.90   2.6.91   6.6.91   27.6.91   16.7.91

58

near Me and please Me ♡ ΙΧΘΥΣ ⃝∞

22.2.93
"Correct us, Yahweh, gently, not in Your
anger or You will reduce us to nothing"
Jr 10:24

Vassula, messenger follows close on messenger,
to tell the world to repent; I am mani-
festing Myself like never before to bring
everyone from far away, back to Me and
follow My Commandments; at any moment
this little flame flickering inside this generation would die down if I do not intervene; even to this day they refuse to

59

hear and believe; the greater they think
they are the less they are in My Eyes,
how could they find favour with Me
when they obstruct My Holy Spirit? what I
hear from them is: "who has authority
over me?" "I am self-sufficient;" My
compassion is great but My severity is as
great ♡ My wrath is as powerful as
My forgiveness; My temples* have now a
common ground with traders; they have
exchanged My Holiness for a tribute to
Satan! I am speaking of those who

* I understood: souls

60

apostatized and have allowed a lie to
pass their lips and now they intend to
compel everyone to be branded with that
lie and I am tired of bearing them;
in My House once, integrity lived there,
since My Law was their daily bread, but
look at what My House has become now,
a desolation, a haunt for the lizard
and the spider! ah .... but I will
undo all this; My Heart is broken
within Me, My child, and My angels
dread and tremble for the Hour I reserved

61

to break out when My orders will be given;
I cannot endure any more to see your Holy
Mother's Tears shed over and over again
every time My Son is recrucified; your generation's sins are leading My Son to Calvary
every moment; together in one voice the
world is blaspheming My Holy Spirit and
all the powers of heaven; daily, the
world is provoking Me: " look! look what
has become of the great Lord's House?" they
say, while tearing It down and dissembling
then, My Soul cannot bear any longer

62

the groans of My Son being recrucified,
although both My Son and your Holy
Mother muffle as best they could their
pain, My Ears hear everything; My Ears
and My Eyes are not human and nothing
escapes Me; since it is your generation that
makes the choice, not I,* the Rebellion in
My House will bring down on you My wrath
and the deepest Darkness is wrought on
earth soon; it is not My choice but yours;
I had chosen to lift you from your graves
with Mercy and Love, Compassion

* That is: instead of choosing God's Peace we chose
to pass into the new era by God's Chastisement.

63

and Peace, but look how so many of you
are unmoved by My offer; nothing can
touch you any longer; My Patience you have
exhausted and you, daughter, be My Echo;
hard as they may harass you, I shall
not allow them to overcome you; on the
contrary, you will be like a sword when
you will pronounce My words; remind them
again that I take pleasure, not in the death
of a wicked and rebellious man, but in
the turning back of a wicked and rebellious
man who changes his ways to win life; this

64

earth that you know will vanish soon,* I
-have decided to hasten My Plan because
of the great sins your generation conceives;
all will vanish, all will wear out
like a garment;*² this will be My way of
destroying the defilement of sin, and
you will realize that from the beginning you were My sacred temples and that
My Spirit was living in you; Ah! for
this Baptism by Fire!! pray and fast
in these last days; I Am is near you ♡

1+2
* Heb. 1: 11
Ap 21 : 1+4

Α ☧ Ω

1

1. 3. 93

'Lord, when Your words came to me,
- I devoured them: Your word is my delight
and the joy of my heart, for I was
called by Your Name, Yahweh, God
Almighty.' (Jr 15:16) I had my eyes
veiled and I did not see You nor Your
Splendour nor Your Glory. Suddenly, in
the deepest depths of my obscurity a Light
shone! Stupefied and stunned by Its
brightness I staggered, ... and the spirit
of lethargy encamping my soul, overwhelmed
by Your Spirit, ceased breathing in me.
    I saw You standing there, silent ....
and it was as if I knew You, Beloved.
    Then, You opened Your Lips, a
Name was given me, and instantly the memory
of my soul was restored; the veil from my eyes
dropped and I found my soul succumbing into my
Father's Arms; O God! How Precious You are to me!

I am Holy; I said: I shall cleanse you
and give you a new heart and put a

2

new spirit in you; I shall remove the spirit
of lethargy from your soul and put My
Spirit in you; on that day I swore to
make you Mine; I swore to heal you and
like a tree, bear fruit for My people; I
swore to fill the starved and every mouth,
yes! I swore to come to you, and turn to
you to till you and sow in your Nothingness My Glory; and now I, God encamped
your soul forever ♡ so prophesy without
fear; go to the dry bones and I
will give them flesh, I will give them

3

breath to praise Me and glorify Me; yes,
I will breathe on the dead so that they
live and shout: "who is like unto God?" I
will remind them that greater love than
their Creator's they shall not find ♡

2. 3. 93

peace be with you ♡ every minute of your
life consecrate for Me, the Sacred Heart,
today, My Vassula, I tell you: live as though
it is your last day on earth; you must do
everything you can to live holy ♡ any
infringement of My Law from your part

4

will be a horror in My Eyes! have you
understood, My Vassula, a horror .... subject
to sin, do not ever abandon My rules;
every offering given with love to Me will
be used for the salvation of souls; subject
to weakness, lean on Me and trust in My
Eternal Power; be rooted in My Sacred Heart
to obtain strength and light; look, have I
not favoured you to reveal My Face to you and
to show all the Treasures of My Sacred Heart?
this Glory of My Church? and by revealing
My Face to you I have revealed It to

5

millions of others ♡ Jesus is My Name and
you are Mine, forever, and now I will name
you after My Passion : <u>Vassula-of-Jesus'-
Passion</u> ♡ and now, Vassula-of-My-Passion
pray with Me for this time of Lent is
going to be heavy on Me ; address yourself
to the Father and say after Me these
words :
                    Eternal Father,
        may Your Name be hallowed,
      to know You is eternal <u>Life</u>,
    to know You is to know the <u>Truth</u>,

6

Father of all Wisdom, sanctify me
    with Your Holy Spirit so that
my heart will utter sayings full
                of wisdom;
            Unique and Perfect,
        Source of Sublime Love,
Your Majesty, ravish my heart to
    praise You night and day ;
Fountain of Myrrh and Aloes,
    fragrance my wretched soul
        with Your delicate fragrance so
that when I meet My King and

7

            Your Beloved Son,
He will not turn His Eyes away from me ;
    to know You is to be in Your Light,
this Light which will show me
                the <u>Way</u>
    and draw me in Your Beloved
            Son's Footsteps ;
    Well of Living Water, come,
    come and immerse me your child
in Your Stream that flows profusely
            out of Your Sanctuary ;
    O God ! I love You to tears !

8

let my wretched soul long for
        all that is Holy,
    let my soul taste Your Tenderness,
Yahweh, You are my God,
        I praise Your Name,
for You have looked upon my wretched
    soul and filled it with the
    brightness of Your Glory ;
    my heart sings to You Father,
my spirit rejoices in Your Spirit ;
    O God, my Father,
allow my soul to succumb in Your

9

Loving Arms

by setting Your Seal on my heart
now, so that my love for
You becomes stronger
than Death itself ; amen

be like a spring, My child, to water
arid lands ♡

God Almighty, allow my soul to take
root in You. I have found true Peace in
You Father. Yahweh, my Lord,
Sovereign from the beginning; evening,
morning, noon, I love, I thirst for the
Holy One whose Finger touched my
heart and with one single of His
Glances ravished my heart. Lord, I stand
before You now, pitiful to look at,

10

prisoner still of this wilderness, come to my
side, for so many persecutors ransom
me ....

be like a tree that is planted by water
springs, unattended you are not; I
Myself am Your Keeper ♡

Loudly I cry to my Saviour now,
Jesus!
Sacred Heart!
You who have plunged my soul in a
baptism of Love, do not let my
soul fail You!

I am Your Keeper too ♡ I am known to
defend the poorest and ♡ save them from
their oppressors, to you My Cup I have

11

passed to drink it with Me .... do you know
why I have come to you? do not be afraid,
peace be with you; I have come to you to
pour out on this generation through you My
Infinite Love; I have also come to remind you
that the Prince of Peace is coming; by the
road He had left He shall return; I will
come is as certain as the dawn; I have
also come to tell everyone what is written
in the Book of Truth,* and explain to you
in simple words what you have not

* I understood, the Scriptures.

12

understood; My Father favoured you to bear
with Me the Cross of Unity and Reconciliation
and cross this desert with Me, side by side;
the Almighty has done great things for
you; I will make My Voice be heard everywhere in spite of the oppositions; listen,
Vassiliki, on account of the impressive
wounds done to you by your accusers who in
reality are My accusers, your compensation will
be great in heaven; I cannot spare you that
favour;* My Justice will rise at its

* Jesus means that by allowing them to attack me, they
make me a favour because heaven will repay me,
compensating me.

13

peak with these traders,*' for indeed they are those traders who apostatized My Church, they have traded the Truth for a lie; My Eyes see everything and My Ears hear everything; I have seen horrors in My sanctuary by

* Traders: My Canadian accusers, in this context.
  Traders: Persecutors of the Holy Spirit.
  Traders: Symbolically meaning: "the jackals" working by night."
  Traders: can represent the second beast of the Ap. 13, meaning ecclesiastical freemasonry.
  Traders: the rationalistic spirit, apostatized and dry.
  Traders: biblical term for a person who traded the Truth for a Lie. It also means: the spirit of rebellion, the false teachers and false prophets of today that Jesus warned us of in the last days to come — St Paul said: "Therefore we teach, not in the way in which philosophy is taught, but in the way that the Spirit teaches us: 'we teach spiritual things spiritually.'"
  (1 Co 2: 13)

14

those very ones who accuse you, pray for their souls, My child; deceit is their principle of behaviour; oh no, they have not reconciled; they never pause to consider that I know about all their wickedness! their hearts are blazing like a fierce flame in the excitement of their plot to consume you together with My Messages; they conspire together*; it is, daughter, only self - interest that makes them want to drown My Voice that comes through you! fraud and oppression fill their mouth; they may bend

* I understood that they are in one clan.

15

their bow and take aim at you, but the weapons they prepared will kill them one after the other unless they repent and make peace with Me; I tell these traders: "your wealth will be seized .... and dressed in terror, you will sit on the ground naked; if you renounce all the sins you have committed, you will be forgiven; there is not much time left! abstain from doing evil and return to Me; why are you so anxious to die Trader? I take no pleasure in abasing you, you who come from My House - repent and you shall live!

16

the Hand of the Father is held out in bless- ing over all who seek Him, Trader; fast plead with the Father for His favour and He will listen "♡ and you daughter, I tell you: stand firm♡, be strong and continue to be My Echo; be like a double-edged sword and proclaim My Message with force and zeal; pray for the conversion of the world with your heart so that the nations recognize the Tenderness of My Holy Spirit; let them see My Love, My Peace, My Patience, My Mercy, and My Fidelity through these Messages,

17

- be fearless and have in mind that I am with you and before you; embrace My Cross which will lead you to heaven; enliven My Church and delight My Soul; go in peace and do your other minor duties; invite Me to share them with you; I Jesus bless you; bless Me and praise Me; ΙΧΘΥΣ ⊃○⊃

Blessed be the Lord. Praised be the Lord, Jesus.

9. 3. 93

Maranatha! Come!

I give you My Peace ♡ I am near, at your very gates My beloved! take My parable of

18

the fig tree: as soon as its twigs grow supple and its leaves come out, you know that summer is near; so with you when you see all these things: know that I am near, at the very gates; as for that day and hour, nobody knows it, neither the angels of heaven, nor the Son, no one but the Father only;* creation! how I longed to gather you all, as a hen gathers her chicks under her wings, and so many of you still refuse! you

* Mt 24: 32 - 36

19

cannot say later on that I have not taken all ways to gather you all in My Sacred Heart to tell you that greater love than Mine you will not find; but you continue to err in this wilderness on your own; I shall be coming soon upon you; I am now sending you messenger after messenger to shout the news; be awake!

Lord, I am happy and filled with joy, maranatha!

do not be afraid; I watch each breath of yours with tender care! in this time of lent

20

I tell you this: preach, My dove, preach and prophesy and pay no heed when your accusers analyze and judge you wrongly; love and be patient; tell Me, My child, can a word or a sentence from the Holy Scriptures be taken out of its context and analized on its own?   No Lord, for it may appear to contradict another word or sentence, said by You.

then neither can one do this thing with these Messages; I have said that I alone am the only lawgiver and judge;* Vassula, let your

* James 4: 12

21

eyes and heart seek only for things that are invisible, the eternal glory is in the invisible things; how I rejoice in poverty and weakness! learn that the teachings I am giving you are for your salvation, and for your freedom, for where My Spirit is, there is freedom ♡ <u>I, the Lord, am Spirit</u>;*¹ write: *²

"If the soul has its own embodiment, so does the spirit have its own embodiment; the first man, Adam, as scripture says, became a living soul; but the last Adam

*¹ Jn. 4: 24
2 Co, 3: 18

*² The Lord asked me to copy a passage He indicated to me from Scriptures.

22

has become a life-giving spirit. that is, first the one with the soul, not the spirit, and after that, the one with the spirit; the first man, being from the earth, is earthly by nature; the second man is from heaven; as this earthly man was, so are we on earth; and as the heavenly man is, so are we in heaven; and we, who have been modelled on the earthly man, will be modelled on the heavenly man. flesh and blood cannot inherit the kingdom of God: and the perishable cannot inherit what lasts for ever; I will

23

tell you something that has been secret: that we are not all going to die, but we shall all be changed; this will be instantaneous in the twinkling of an eye, when the last trumpet sounds; it will sound, and the dead will be raised, imperishable, and we shall be changed as well, because our present perishable nature must put on imperishability and this mortal nature must put on immortality; when this perishable nature has put on imperishability, and when this mortal nature has put on

24

immortality, then the words of Scripture will come true: Death is swallowed up in victory; Death, where is your victory? Death where is your sting? now the sting of death is sin, and sin gets its power from the Law. so let us thank God for giving us the victory through our Lord Jesus Christ;"* yes, I have set you free from the law of sin and death ♡ come, remain faithful to Me until your race is over; I, your Creator, shall finish it with you; with Me, you

* 1 Co 15: 44-57

25

should not fear; with Me your table shall
be full; ♡ I shall never desert you;

A ☧ Ω

15.3.93

Vassula of My Passion, keep your eyes on Me;
delight Me and give as you gave* yesterday;
lean on Me always and your mouth will
be used as My Sword; I love you; be
one with Me; IΧΘΥΣ ⋯⟨⟩

* At ARLES in France, during the meeting.

26

17.3.93

Peace be with you; My child, you are to
teach My children all that I have given you;
do not fear for I am in front of you and
I am your Shield; no one will ever, no
matter how much the evil one tries, come between you and Me; although Satan mobi-
lizes men to handicap you, and although
he makes them join forces against you, never
fear; I am the Almighty and My Eyes
witness the injustice done to you; beloved,
I will imbue you with My Strength and I

27

will give to all My children bread in abundance ♡ I will make your zeal for My
House devour My enemies; I will make you
a threat to them; so never fear, since I
Am is standing in front of you; My blessings are upon you and every fibre of your
heart will be covered by Courage, Strength
and Peace; in this way you will atone for
the salvation of souls and for the renewal
of My House in the most perfect way ♡
lift your voice without fear and prophesy;
prophesy, My child, to blot out wickedness

28

from so many hearts! let those who have
ears let them listen to what the Spirit
today is saying to the churches; let all
who are thirsty come: write and tell My
sacerdotal souls this: "rebellion is at its
work already, but in secret, and the one
who is holding it back has first <u>to be re-
moved</u>, before the Rebel appears openly;"*
I tell you, love My Church as I love Her
and as I sacrificed Myself for My Church
to make Her entirely holy, you too, My

* 2 Th 2:7

29

priests, sacrifice yourselves to Her, imitate Me; I am telling you all this and I know that My sheep who belong to Me will listen to My Voice and will never fail Me, I am addressing you today to tell you from the core of My Heart the same embittered words I uttered at My Last Supper around My disciples: " someone who shares My table rebels against Me; I tell you this now, before it happens, so that when it does happen you may believe that I am He speaking, today; " My little children, do not let your hearts

30

be troubled, trust in Me, and do not fear; soon a Baptism of Fire will be sent by the Father to burn the crimes of this world; the hour will come when men of power will enter My Sanctuary, men who do not come from Me; in fact this hour is already here; I, Jesus Christ, wish to warn My priests, bishops and cardinals, I wish to warn all My House of a great tribulation; My Church is approaching a great tribulation; remember, I have chosen you, by My sanctifying Spirit to glorify Me; I have

31

chosen you from the beginning to be the sturdy pillars of My Church and to live by faith in the Truth ♡ I have chosen you to share My Glory and to shepherd My lambs; I tell you solemnly that you will soon be tested by fire: pray and fast so as not to be put to the test; stand firm and <u>keep</u> the traditions you were taught; <u>obey My pope*</u> no matter what comes up; remain faithful to him and I will give you the graces and the strength you will

* John Paul II

32

need; I urge you to <u>keep faithful to him</u> and keep away from anyone who rebels against him; above all, <u>never listen to anyone who dispels him</u>; never let your love for him grow insincere; soon you will be faced with an ordeal as you have never experienced before; My enemies will try to buy you for themselves with insidious speeches, the evil one is at his work already and Destruction is not far away from you; the pope* will have much to suffer; this

* John Paul II

33

is why you will all be persecuted for proclaiming the Truth and for being obedient to My pope; this is also why they will hate you, because their deeds are evil and indeed, everybody who works for evil hates the Light and avoids it, for fear his actions of Destructiveness should be exposed; I tell you solemnly, every fibre of My Heart is lacerated; if anyone comes your way bringing a different doctrine than the one I Myself instituted, do not listen to him; these people come from the Deceiver ♡

34

I have laid down My foundation on Peter, the rock .... and the gates of the underworld can never hold out against it ... if anyone comes your way and tells you : " move from your fidelity you have for this pope to another's sound movement"; do not move! beware! the yeast of the Deceiver may be powerful and might taste good, but in reality it is of <u>deadly deception</u>! do not allow anyone to deceive you; resist the devil's tactics, for today, My priests, you will have to conquer evil with the strength

35

you receive from Me who am the Truth; you will be in a spiritual war as never before with an army which originates from the powers of Darkness; pray, My beloved ones, all the time; I Am is with you; I love you all; a man could have had no greater love than to have laid down his life for his friends, as I have; you are My friends; be sincere with one another, love one another and stand firm without fear when the great Tribulation, that now hovers like a black cloud over My House

36

will cover it like a black veil ♡ I have told you all this now before ♥ it happens, so that when it happens you may believe;

ΙΧΘΥΣ ⊰≻≺⊱

True Life in God - Presentation by Vassula
Franciscan Prayer Center, Independence, MO, January 11-12, 1992

True Life in God
Video and Audio Tape 1 (1 ½ hours)
- detailed account of Vassula's background and conversion
- how she receives Jesus' Messages
- readings from Messages include God's Love for us and Church Unity.
- Purification Message: *"Your eyes unveiled...then a breathe will slide over your face and the powers of Heaven will shake...your souls will see what they had once seen...they will see the most tender Father."*
- readings include Messages from the Blessed Mother Mary:
- *"God will be coming to you but you do not know in which way."*
- *"Your prayer can change the world; pray to obtain God's Mercy."*

True Life in God
Video and Audio Tape 2 (2 hours)
- Vassula gives brief introduction, including family.
- Vassula reads messages on Church Unity, Grace, Prayer, Purification, Shortness of Time, the Chastisements, the Present Dark Era, and *"This is a time of great mercy."*
- Jesus directs us to pray for the intentions of the Sacred Heart of Jesus and the Immaculate Heart of Mary.
- Jesus begs us not to permit any rivals for His Love; Let no thought, no desire, no opinion, no plan rival His Love.
- Question and Answer session addresses Satan, Heaven, Hell, corporal works of Mercy, Church Unity.

True Life in God Highlights
Video (only) Tape 3 (1 hour)

- highlights from the Independence presentation including the story of her background, conversion, and how she receives Jesus' Messages.
- Messages including Church Unity, Grace, and Prayer
- Question and Answer session on the Messages and their meaning
- comments from Fr. Joseph Meisburger and Fr. Santan Pinto.

Respect for Life
Video (only) Tape 4 (30 minutes)

Vassula and Fr. James Fannan are interviewed by Mike McDonald of the **Life Matters** TV Program in Detroit.

- Two Messages from the Father, one from the Sacred Heart, and one from Our Lady:

- *"The Father is strongly opposed to abortion and He shares how much He is hurt by it. Still there is His Mercy if we repent."*

Alliance of the Two Hearts
Audio (only) Tape 3

Interview with Vassula by Fr. Michael O'Carroll, November, 1991, London. Messages include:
- *"The inner power of my Church is My Holy Spirit, that transfigures, uplifts...and makes out of your spirit ... living torches of light to proclaim, without fear, My Word."*
- *"From my Sacred Heart I will perform at the End of Times, works as never before."*
- Blessed Mother calls us to rebuild His primitive Church inside our hearts.

Vassula Addresses the World Council of Churches Ecumenical Conference
Audio (only) Tape 4 - Geneva

Vassula, invited by this Council to present the Messages of Jesus regarding Church Unity, reads these messages:
- *"Tell them that he who maintains to be just, yet remains divided, will eat from the fruit he has sown and will perish."*
- *"Tell those who want to hear that: unless they lower their voices, they will never hear Mine."*
- *"Unite! Assemble! Invoke My Name together!"*
- *"Yet, if you come to Me as you are, I can heal you, ... and you will glorify Me."*
- *"My Church will be rebuilt inside your hearts and you will acknowledge each other as your brother in your heart."*

Note: Transcripts from Audio tapes 3 and 4 are printed in Volumes IV and V respectively.

Trinitas™
P.O. Box 475
Independence, MO, USA 64051-0475

Office Address: 16400 E. Truman Road
Independence, MO, USA 64050-4191

Phone Orders:
(816) 254-4489 • Fax: (816) 254-1469

Sold to:

Name _____

Address _____

City _____

State _____ Zip _____

Phone _____

Please charge my credit card: ❏ Visa ❏ M/C

Card Number _____

Expiration Date _____

Signature _____

discounts available for Bookstores and Religious Goods Stores

Item	Quantity	Price	Amount
"True Life in God" Volume I		9.95	
"True Life in God" Volume II		9.95	
"True Life in God" Volume III		9.95	
"True Life in God" Volume IV		9.95	
"True Life in God" Volume V		6.75	
"True Life in God" Volume VI		8.50	
"True Life in God" Video 1 - 90 minutes		14.00	
"True Life in God" Video 2 - 2 hours		15.00	
"True Life in God" Video 3 - 1 hour		13.00	
"Respect for Life" Video 4 - 30 minutes		12.00	
"True Life in God" Audio 1		5.00	
"True Life in God" Audio 2		6.00	
"Alliance of the Two Hearts" Audio 3		5.00	
"World Council of Churches" Audio 4		5.00	

Shipping and Handling

1-2	$2.00 per item	
3-5	$4.50 total	
6-8	$6.00 total	

extra shipping charges outside continental U.S.

Sub-total	
Sales Tax @ 5.975% MO Residents only	
➡ Shipping + Handling	

Submit in U.S. Funds only | Total |